Animal Disorders

Animal Disorders
Essays on Trans-Species Relationships

Deborah Thompson

www.blacklawrence.com

Executive Editor: Diane Goettel
Cover Design: Zoe Norvell
Cover Art: "Snout #1" by Deborah Williams
Book Design: Amy Freels

Published 2021 by Black Lawrence Press.
Printed in the United States.

Contents

Introduction

A man cages lions and tigers in his backyard. A woman's house teems with so many cats that she's lost count and doesn't even notice when one dies. A man longing to become one with bears gets devoured by one.

"Animal Disorders," I call them, these enactments, by a select few individuals, of much more widespread cultural disorders. These extreme versions of unhealthy relationships with animals capture irreconcilable contradictions and impossibilities in our approaches to (non-human) animals that we otherwise manage to repress.

More mundane contradictions abound, often unnoticed. Millions of people who condemn cockfighting will eat the carcasses of chickens that were crammed into cages and de-beaked to keep them from pecking each other to death during their short lives. Our culture euthanizes hundreds of thousands of unwanted dogs every year while spending millions of dollars on a wanted few. Researchers "sacrifice" one dog to save another. An animal rights advocate may condemn animal cruelty in research laboratories but receive radiation therapy treatments first tested out on beagles. A woman who considers herself a vegetarian feeds her dogs meat.

These are some of the everyday symptoms of animal disorders that I find myself in. What follows are personal essays exploring disordered relationships with animals on the part of myself and of my (human) culture. I would characterize myself as having a fairly representative case of early-stage animal disorder. I'm the woman referred to above, the one who considers herself a vegetarian but feeds her dogs meat. I'm not (quite) (yet) a hoarder, and I don't live among bears or run with wolves, but just a small change in a variable or two of my life might produce a very different story.

You may hear in my term "animal disorders" the echo of other disorders, like "sleep disorders" or "eating disorders." Feminist philosopher Susan Bordo has proposed that eating disorders—anorexia nervosa, bulimia, binge eating, orthorexia, etc.—are "crystallizations of culture." Their symptoms make manifest not just individual psyches but also cultural ailments. Eating disorders emerged historically at a time when Western culture's approaches to food, consumption, and women's bodies clashed. The individuals who developed eating disorders were primarily women responding to impossibly contradictory cultural demands: *Eat! But don't eat! Consume everything, but restrain yourself! You deserve to indulge yourself, but your worth comes from denying yourself!* Their disordered eating forms a compromise among irreconcilable desires and demands.

Such compromised conditions similarly underlie sleep disorders. We find ourselves whirling in a culture of perpetual motion and simultaneity, a fast culture of fast food for fast company, with speedy motors and instant messaging, a culture that never sleeps. We desperately need sleep so that we can perform better-stronger-faster, but who has time for sleep? So our culture proliferates amphetamines to keep us up and opiates to push us through the pain. In such a culture, it's inevitable that some people will develop insomnia and irregular sleep cycles. Some even develop a fear of sleeping. Others develop addictions to uppers or downers. Such disordered individuals are themselves symptoms of larger cultural disorders in the body politic. In their extreme and dramatic versions, they embody anxieties and untenable contradictions latent in the culture at large.

So too with animal disorders. When it comes to both domesticated and wild animals, we make ourselves oxymorons. We are a culture whose approach to our non-human kin is contradictory. As psychologist Hal Herzog puts it so eloquently in his book of the same title, "Some we love, some we hate, some we eat." And some we love to death.

In this era of mass extinctions, we long to connect with the dying wild, even though acting on that longing may hasten the extinction. We become lovers of a "nature" that's harmed by our consumption of it. Our culture produces a Terry Thompson, raising endangered tigers in an Ohio backyard, and then setting them free into an urban safari, as I explore in "The Other Thompson." Or we create a Timothy Treadwell, destroyed by and destroying the grizzly bear he longs to become. Maybe we express our love for wild animals by hunting them, or seek oneness with nature by capturing its inhabitants. Or maybe we're just nature voyeurs, viewing wilderness vistas on our screensavers while carbonating the atmosphere with our air conditioners.

We're a bundle of animal contradictions. We'll do anything to save some animals while casually obliterating others. We treat some animals more "humanely" than we treat some humans while killing others just for sport. We can't seem to figure out even the legal, much less the ethical, status of animals. We can't figure out whether domestic animals are objects we own or wards we steward. We don't know how to value nature—or even what nature is.

Like eating and sleep disorders, animal disorders come in many forms. Indeed, there's even some overlap between the two, such as when extreme veganism masks a fear of food. But might our "ordinary" approach to eating meat, or our acceptance of factory farms, or our alienation from the means of meat production, be just as disordered?

While mass extinction and factory farms are relatively new, animal disorders are as old as *Homo sapiens*, as timeless as myth. They are not, I recognize, merely culture-bound, but universal. Just look at the many myths across human cultures of human-animal hybrids: the elephant-headed god Ganesha, the jackal god Anubis, all those centaurs and minotaurs, fauns and satyrs, mermaids and mermen, not to mention Spiderman and Batman and Catwoman. Or look at the array of legends where humans are engulfed inside nonhuman animals: Jonah and the whale, Little Red Riding Hood. Or the many tales of becoming-animal: Actaeon, the hunter of Greek myth who became the hunted, turned by

Artemis into a deer and torn apart by his dogs; Arachne, the talented weaver who, in her hubris, challenged Athena (thereby claiming superhuman powers) and was turned into a spider; Philomela, raped by her brother-in-law, who then cut out her tongue so she couldn't tell her tale, was transformed into a nightingale forever singing her lament. Myths world-wide attest to active questioning about human-animal relations. Every human culture, I would venture, has its animal disorders. However, like unhappy families, every culture has been disordered in its own way. I sometimes wonder if twenty-first-century U.S. culture is so enmeshed in its animal disorders that it doesn't even know how to dream of recovery.

This book is not about every culture, nor does it venture to present a comprehensive view even of twenty-first-century U.S. culture. Instead, it offers my own particular versions of animal disorders over the past fifty-odd years of my middle-class American culture. I have both objectified and anthropomorphized animals, sometimes simultaneously ("Consider the Hamster"; "Pack Theory"). I've displayed hoarding tendencies ("The Other Thompson") and have benefited from animal experiments that I condemn ("Schrödinger's Dogs"). I have generated my own personal myths of metamorphosis, which I've believed while disbelieving ("The Blue Heron Returns"). While overlooking the slow violence of environmental devastation and habitat destruction, I've grieved both *with* and *through* individual animals ("Big Cats"; "The Meaning of Meat"; "For the Polar Bears") as well as *for* animals ("A Bitchuary"). The essays that follow deliver dispatches from one representative sufferer of animal disorders.

1/ Consider The Hamster

As I shuffle my cart toward the dog food aisle in the maze of a mega-pet store, a golden glow draws me to the Small Animal zone. It's the translucent yellow acrylic of a hamster hut catching the fluorescent rays. Inhaling the long-ago scent of cedar chips, I peer through a glass display case labeled *Golden Hamster, Male. $15.99*. I spy a mound of tan fur exposed above the shallow bedding. Like many Americans of my late-baby-boomer generation, I had hamsters as a child. In 1970, keeping hamsters as pets was a fairly new phenomenon, but gaining momentum. Back then, it seemed the most natural thing in the world. Now, the yellow fluorescence casts the practice in an alien light, and prods me to reconsider the hamster.

My first pet, when I was a seven-year-old girl in 1970, was my hamster Frisky. I'd wanted a dog, like the Klingers' gentle collie next door, but my brother's allergies made this impossible. At the pet store I chose a hamster over a gerbil because the gerbil's tail looked too wormy—yuck—and because my father told me that the hamster could store food in his cheek pouches, then paw it back out. Frisky was five inches of waistless waddle, earnest-eyed, and all mine. My father helped me set up the clear plastic Habitrail cage in my bedroom. The box housed a red plastic wheel and a lone translucent yellow tower. Dad showed me how to change the water bottle, food trough, and, once a week, the wood-chip bedding that filled with doll-house-sized poops. At night I fell asleep to the thrum of the spinning wheel, and when I woke up from a nightmare the steady churning calmed me back to oblivion.

In the daytime I nudged the groggy hamster awake and cupped him in my hand to hold his warmth. I offered him a sunflower seed between the pinch of my index finger and thumb; I liked to feel the slight tug in my fingertips as he took it and to hear the crack as he busily opened the shell and extracted the meat. Sometimes I coaxed him to stand on hind legs in begging position, or covered his head to feel his soft pink paws burrowing a tunnel between my thumb and index finger. When I set him down he ran for crevices until I scooped him up again. Because he delighted in cardboard tunnels, I used way more toilet paper than I needed just to empty the roll faster. Above all, I liked to stroke his fur from head to tail-stump as he bowed under my fingers. I imagined that Frisky appreciated my ministrations, and that he and I shared a bond. Behind his delicate, hyperactive nose, his rich black eyes reflected my love, just as nature intended.

As a hamster-owner in 1970, I typified my cultural moment. Now, however, as I poke into hamster's labyrinthine journey to pet-dom, the story shifts, and I find, instead, a most unnatural history.

Hamsters hail from the Middle East and Asia. Although these elusive but prevalent desert-dwellers must have been noticed earlier, they weren't mentioned in writing until 1774, and only received a scientific name in 1839 by Englishman George Robert Waterhouse. Having acquired a specimen (probably dead, though accounts are fuzzy) from Aleppo, Syria, Waterhouse named it for the golden hue of its pelt and presented it to the London Zoological Society as a new species, the *Cricetus auratus* (now *Mesocricetus auratus*). Waterhouse's specimen can still be viewed today, as Item BM(NH) 1855.12.24.120, at the National History Museum in London.

Even after this "discovery," hamsters' interactions with human beings remained limited for nearly another century; the rodents, if noted at all, were regarded as nuisances for their ability to invade granaries, hoard husks and seeds in their cheeks, and bury them later in underground pantries, sometimes containing upwards of 50 pounds of food. Impoverished laborers in China have actually survived famines by unearthing hamsters' hoards.

Hamsters proved themselves more useful to humans in the realm of medical research. In the 1920s, scientists discovered that the Chinese dwarf hamster was easily infected with the protozoan causing the human disease Leishmaniasis (marked by skin lesions and organ damage). They wanted to exploit hamsters as research specimens, but found this species difficult to breed in the lab. So the hunt was on for breedable hamsters.

In 1930, a Jewish biologist in Jerusalem (then under the Turkish empire) resolved to track down and breed the Syrian hamster. Israel Aharoni and his team eventually succeeded, but the attempt was fraught with problems that would recur in my own household forty years later. His team finally located, eight feet below ground in a wheat field in Aleppo, a mother and her ten pups. But once placed in a box, the mother ate one of the pups and had to be "restrained"—in a bottle of cyanide—from further infanticide. To this hapless Eve can be traced the genetic line of nearly all domesticated Syrian hamsters today.

The nine pups were then taken to Jerusalem and eye-dropper-fed into childhood. Alas, five hamsters chewed their way out of the wood-bottomed cage, and soon escaped. That left four hamsters, one of them male, who then ate one of the females. And then there were three. The researchers finally separated the remaining three and eventually got the brother to mate with one of his sisters. That litter was the first of 150 offspring from the incestuous pair, and those offspring multiplied, and the multiples multiplied. From thence came the domestic hamster tribe.

I don't think my father, himself a proud Jew and a scientist, knew that a Jewish scientist was responsible for the Syrian hamster diaspora. If he had, he would have been pleased. Of course, we didn't call them *Syrian* hamsters. I doubt that such epithet omission was confined to my pro-Israel family. *Syrian* would not have played well in the 1970s U.S. Pet store labels read *Golden* or sometimes *Teddy Bear*, and hamsters' origins and history went unlabeled. To me, it was as if the hamsters miraculously appeared out of nowhere, or as if they were mass-produced in factories overseas, like most of my toys. It never occurred to me, as a child, to ask where they came from. They came from the store.

When the FDA formed in 1937, the agency required all commercial pharmaceuticals to be tested on laboratory animals. The demand for Aharoni's hamsters increased. The age of animal experimentation was on, and hamsters, along with mice, rats, rabbits, guinea pigs, and other rodents, were favored subjects—so much so that a whole industry arose to breed them on a mass scale. Ironically, hamsters' incestuous lineage makes them prime research subjects, as they show little genetic variation. This in-breeding also makes them particularly susceptible to the congenital heart diseases so eagerly studied in medical laboratories. Although the guinea pig bears the metaphorical weight, the hamster bears a significant portion of the actual burden of medical research.

Hamsters went from the lab to the home—sometimes literally, carried out in pockets. We still refer to them as "pocket pets." Pet stores began selling them in the 1940s, the waning days of the caged-bird craze. Indeed, many of the early pet hamsters were kept in revamped birdcages. By the 1970s, hamsters' popularity boomed, especially as starter pets for young children. Hamster-keeping has even been characterized as a childhood rite of passage in North America. Hamsters make good first pets because they're fairly hardy, resistant to disease, relatively low-maintenance, and short-lived. With a life expectancy of approximately two years, they rarely outlive their owner's childhood, and often don't outlive their novelty. They're also very cute. And, of course, they can easily be kept in cages. They serve as low-stakes trial runs, the guinea pigs of pet-keeping.

While hamsters were first held in birdcages, aquaria, or other makeshift enclosures, the emerging pet industry quickly filled this new niche with specialty hamster merchandise. New developments in polymer technologies allowed the wire cages to be augmented with and even replaced by plastic ones, most famously Habitrail "habitats." Frisky began with the basic Habitrail starter cage, but I soon purchased add-ons with my allowance money. The larger cage tunneled into an annex, which gained a second wheel and a higher look-out tower. Pet stores today carry far more colorful, whimsical, even futuristic options in accessories. The Habitrail OVO resembles a sci-fi spaceship with its multicolored, ovoid living spaces and turrets, its sleek, aerodynamic-looking wheels, and its add-on tunneling systems. Crittertrail offerings range from an all-pink one-level abode (where, I can imagine, Barbie herself might happily reside) to an "Extreme Challenge" playpen for hot-rod hamsters. You can buy a carry-case shaped like a bus, potty pens, even a four-piece Sit-N-Living Room suite, which includes a Hide-N-See television set, so that, when your hamster burrows into it, you can watch him "on television," live and encaged.

My favorite hamster accessory back in the day was the yellow plastic bubble, sometimes called a "run-around" or "roll-about" ball. Once inside it, Frisky started scampering. In my fantasy, he would follow me around like a dog. In reality he kept running into our wood-paneled walls. I now know that hamsters have weak eyesight, and mostly just see contrasts, which Frisky was denied in his yellow translucent sphere. For this reason, today's balls are usually clear. The new run-around tracks allow you to set up elaborate railroad-like loop-de-loops in your living room. You can also buy the balls with training wheels for extra stability. Despite hamsters' being notoriously difficult to sex, Crittertrail offers a pink carriage for girls and a red racing car for boys. Although I didn't have all of these extra embellishments back in the 1970s, I still managed to play out my fantasies on my hamster. As a young consumerist-in-training, I practiced accessorizing, rehearsing the American Dream of the ever-expanding house.

One day, in spite of my better judgment, I allowed my learning-disabled older brother to hold Frisky. As soon as I lowered Frisky into David's cupped hands, the hamster tried to bolt. David squeezed the tiny body harder. Frisky bit David's finger. David panicked and threw Frisky against the wall.

My next hamster, Squeaky, arrived with a new room for the growing hamster mansion, along with additional salt licks and wood chews. My father built a wooden maze with a removable chicken-wire cover, and we held inconclusive "training sessions." I never let David hold any of my hamsters again. I couldn't protect his various gerbils, mice, and rats over the years, but I could protect my hamsters, to whom I was determined to give the perfect life. I cut down old vanilla wafer boxes into hamster huts, which Squeaky then customized with his compulsive chewing. I even ate carrots so he could get the peelings. My father challenged me to think like a hamster, so I tried to imagine how it would be to see very little, but to hear ultrasonic wavelengths, and to smell everything, even the walls. I wondered at Squeaky's ever-working pink nose, at how it could feel shapes through scent the way our fingers do through touch. Mostly, though, I related to my hamsters much like I did to my stuffed animals.

After Frisky and Squeaky came Goldie, to whom I remember reciting my speech on *tzedakah*—charity—for the temple speech contest. (I came in second place, having lost to an oratory on reconciling the Bible with Evolution.) Then came Pinky, Piglet, and finally Hamlet. The configuration of cages got more and more elaborate, expanding into a compound more than a castle. When it outgrew my bedroom we moved it to the basement. I never stopped to consider how far that locale—cold, damp, dungeon-like—was from the hamster's natural desert habitat.

One night a hamster—I can't remember which one—got loose. My father and I searched into the wee hours. It's one of my most vivid memories, among an ever-dwindling collection, of my father during my childhood. I wore my purple pajamas, my dad his plaid flannel bathrobe. We each wielded a flashlight. Dad explained that the hamster couldn't survive on his own; he'd either starve or be eaten. He needed us. So we should look hard, with "eagle eyes." The hamster, in my prepubescent narrative, was a damsel in distress, and my father the rescuer. Vivid in freeze-frame memory is the climax of this fairy tale, the moment of victory, when my father shone the flashlight behind the General Electric washing machine and framed the hamster in a halo of light. Pinky (or was it Goldie? Or Piglet?) was saved.

Now, though, when I revisit that memory-image forty years later, it's overlaid by the images in Art Spiegelman's graphic novel of the holocaust, *Maus*. Through anthropomorphism, ironically, I come a little closer to thinking in hamster. Those panels of German cats shining flashlights on Jewish mice in their hiding places. The mice's eyes dilated in terror. What if, from the hamster's eyes, my father and I were the SS, not the Jews?

My last hamster died of thirst. It didn't take a necropsy to determine cause of death. Hamlet's neck had rigidified in a desperate outstretch, his mouth pressed to the lip of the water bottle, his last calories of energy undoubtedly used to suck for sustenance. By the time I finally remembered to trudge down to the basement to replenish his food and water, the poor critter might have been dead for days. I was thirteen years old by then, busy with tennis practice and bat mitzvah prep.

Pet-keeping, the story went, teaches children compassion, responsibility, and an ethic of domestic stewardship. That's surely what my father had in mind, though it turned out not to be the case for my poor Hamlet, and probably for many other Hamlets in middle-class, suburban homes across the land. But beyond memories of my abuse of Hamlet, an even more uncomfortable thought now gnaws at me. Maybe it wasn't just Hamlet who suffered in the end, but all of his predecessors, too, even those subjected to my outpourings of love and care. Maybe pet-keeping itself serves to naturalize imprisonment under the name of love.

Soon after I was bat mitzvahed ("batzed"), I began to question Judaism, both as a religion and a culture, and especially to question Israeli politics. I lost the certainty of my childhood, when I could use my allowance money to buy a tree in Israel and dedicate it "To the Jews who died in the Yom Kippur War." Doubts were afoot and beginning to burrow. But I retained—along with a sense of guilt as my default emotion—the teaching that we, as Jews, knowing all too intimately how casually a culture can slip into a holocaust, had a special obligation to be alert to injustice, which can come in many guises. I didn't yet understand, though, how an ideology of injustice has, like hamsters, an uncanny ability to hide, burrowing underground below consciousness.

After I went on to college, my brother continued to keep hamsters. When I visited home one winter break I met his latest, an obese Syrian hamster so ornery that David named him Fussy. One day, my mother and I came home from a shopping trip to find, taped to the front door, a note in my brother's still child-like handwriting: "MRS Fussy just gave birth to 9 yung uns." By the time my mom and I reached the basement, Mrs. Fussy had already cannibalized one of the "young 'uns" and was working on a second.

I now know that hamsters' eating of their newborn pups when stressed is well documented; they are notorious for such infanticide, particularly in the presence of threatening foreign species like humans.

Even my brother, always fascinated with primal violence, had had enough of hamsters.

Decades later, while I've moved on to dogs, American consumption of hamsters rolls on. Some of the Greek Tragedy-like problems with hamsters as pets—fratricide, infanticide, and cannibalism—have resolved with the influx of dwarf hamsters into pet stores. These species are sociable enough to be kept in cages together without the risk of fratricide. But they're still in cages, subjected to our diurnal schedules, while their nocturnal bodies must ache to burrow eight feet underground. That's under the best of circumstances. What happened to Hamlet, or to Frisky and the Fussy family, surely isn't a rarity. An informal survey among my friends yields quite a few "sad hamster stories" (along with sad gerbil, rat, rabbit, and guinea pig tales). Googling hamster abuse reveals mistreatment in laboratories and pet stores too. One video shows a pet store employee nonchalantly scooping dead hamsters out of their display cages and into the garbage.

It gets worse. Laboratory hamsters come in different models, some genetically altered, which can be ordered in bulk from a catalog. They're commonly used in disease cytology, for which blood samples are taken by inserting a capillary pipette into the eye. The cheek pouch can also make a good transplantation site, meaning that very un-cheek-like cells and organs can be observed growing from it. The use of hamsters in laboratory research has declined from a high of over 500,000 in 1976 to well under 200,000 a year in the twenty-first century. But that's still 200,000 Friskies a year. Or Squeakies. Or, alas, poor Hamlets.

The number of hamsters kept as pets is surely much higher. But how much better is their fate? Is keeping hamsters in cages as pets fundamentally different—as I have wanted to believe—from using them as research specimens? The lessons hamster-keeping taught me are hard to unlearn: that living things can be owned, purchased along with the other accessories in the pet store; that they're here to serve my needs; that caging and controlling them is for their own good. Is that compassion? Could hamster-keeping have naturalized animal cruelty under the name of love? And is it too big a leap to notice that the rise of factory farms and the tremendous spike in medical testing on animals coincided with the surge in caged-animal pet-keeping? Or am I going too far?

"Consider the Lobster," David Foster Wallace's famous essay, which inspired me to consider the hamster, begins in a journalistic description of the Maine Lobster Festival and of lobster-eating, before craftily changing tracks. Eventually, Wallace eviscerates common-sense ideology about humans' inherent right to cook and eat lobster, and indeed any sentient living being. The essay climaxes in a series of questions about the very ethics of eating animals: "Is it possible that future generations will regard our present agribusiness and eating practices in much the same way we now view Nero's entertainments or Mengele's experiments?" I find my own observations about keeping hamsters as pets lead me to some similarly inconvenient questions.

The hamster spinning on the wheel became my generation's trope for dead-end work and an unfulfilling life. We identified with her frustration, and used her image to illustrate ours. But why didn't we circle back and think of the hamster? Why didn't we take the metaphor literally, and consider how the hamster herself felt about her wheel-bound, cage-bound predicament? Should we expect her to like it any more than we do? Why didn't we ask ourselves about the ethics of pet-keeping itself? About what gave us the right to put animals in cages for our own amusement?

"It's human nature to want to keep pets," people say when I start to feel my way through this thought maze. "It's the human condition." They—we—also tend to assume that it's "the human condition" to put humans at the center of all considerations; we consider the human almost exclusively, and see this anthropocentrism as natural, as inevitable, and as so common-sensical that it's beneath noting. But the history of hamster-keeping suggests that it wasn't always seen as natural for humans to make hamsters into pets—and, indeed, it might even go against nature. Hamsters as pets arose within a specific ideology of twentieth-century consumerism, when it seemed natural to colonize, import, and own other beings purely for our pleasure. Burrowed, hamster-like, deep underneath our anthropocentric belief in "the human condition" is a much more elusive, light-averse clue into how a human becomes conditioned.

"It's just a hamster," all reasonable people would say, and yes, I know that I'm being more than a bit ridiculous, that the hamster's confinement is quite small on the scale of animal mistreatment, and perhaps not worth worrying about when more urgent abuses—the overcrowding and de-beaking of chickens on factory farms, the use of gestation crates and veal crates for large mammals, and vivisection of primates, for starters—demand our attention. But if we begin by considering the case of the hamster, and if we decide that the undoubtedly genuine enjoyment and companionship we receive from them does not justify caging them, then don't all those other instances become that much more unacceptable? Doesn't it make sense to start small?

On the other hand, if we keep digging down this tunnel, we risk stumbling upon more fundamental beliefs. Every pure and innocent childhood memory, everything we consider natural when it comes to pets and eating and clothing and habitats and human priorities, would be up for reconsideration. Even dog ownership...and here we're getting into dangerous territory, because I can't imagine a life without my dogs—the dogless life is not worth living—so I must now withdraw from this line of questioning. That's farther than I'm able to go. As David Foster Wallace wryly concludes in his consideration of lobsters, "[t]here are limits to what even interested persons can ask of each other."

Any condemnation of hamster-keeping I might voice is further muted by the recalcitrance of desire. When I stand in front of the pet store's brightly-lit hamster display, history and ethics dissolve, and I'm stirred, even now, by old longings, memories of tactile sensations of fur and warmth. One animal advocacy group says that you can enjoy animals without enslaving them; you can, for example, enjoy the squirrel in your backyard without entrapping it. But what's missing in their version is the greediness of touch. Just to hold, in your palm, a beating-hearted thing, soft and warm, furry and nervous. To smooth its angora fur with your fingertips to calm it, to feel so in touch with its slowing beats that the hamster itself becomes a heart in your hands. To feel your fingers wrap around it and call it your own.

2/ Big Cats

Mutual of Omaha's Wild Kingdom featured in my childhood both as my favorite TV show and as my weekly trauma. My father and I watched it together at 5:00 p.m. Sunday evenings, eating our supper on TV trays in the den. Sprouting green shag carpeting and wood-paneled walls, which sported display cases of choice butterflies we caught in the Forest Preserves, the room simulated the woods and jungles that Marlin Perkins trekked. My father, curious about all animals, was most fascinated by the big cats. I nervously chewed a bite of supper as the cheetah leapt, and swallowed hard as she toppled the gazelle.

The first deaths I witnessed were on *Mutual of Omaha's Wild Kingdom*, and they made me wonder how God chose between the starving cheetah and the ailing gazelle. But my father was a scientist, as was his God, and both took an emotionally distant approach to the earth's creatures. Dad reminded me that in the wild, every predator was also prey, and if I felt sad for the fallen wildebeest I should also recognize that the pride of lions got to live another day. That was the natural order of things. It made no sense to be upset with nature. Besides, he explained, animals don't think the way we do. They don't have our moral code, our understanding or ability to ask why, our full emotional palette. I should be careful not to anthropomorphize or sentimentalize.

So I learned how to watch with willed stoicism, forcing myself not to empathize.

My father also taught me the joy of observing details, and of seeing the unexpected. The log in the swamp that shows the faintest outline of a crocodile jaw beneath two eye-bumps. The pink edge of an elephant's ear. The leopard's camouflaging rosettes, which looked to me like a thousand eyes staring.

Ronald Earl Thompson was a scientist to the core, and a scientist very much of his time, situated at the crest of two centuries of rising faith in the Scientific Method. Ever since he was a young boy, my father loved chemistry in particular. Hunching over his A. C. Gilbert chemistry set while reports of WWII crackled over the radio, Ronnie took great pleasure mixing two solutions to make a third, sometimes with a poof of light or heat or color. Against reports of casualties and advertisements to buy war bonds, my father made baking soda volcanoes, turned fire green with boric acid or purple with potassium chloride, and concocted aluminum sulfide stink bombs.

But even more than the minor pyrotechnics, he loved the *discipline* of science. Maybe it was the backdrop of war that made science's stabilities so attractive. He loved that the truth was out there, distinct from us, regardless of how we felt about it, indifferent to our fears or needs. He loved the idea of objectivity—its solidity, its dream of certainty. This scientific method was tough. It required a rigorous resistance to the comforts of interpretation. That challenge was one of the things that made the "hard" sciences, such as chemistry and biology and physics, hard, as opposed to the "soft" social sciences and the even softer arts and humanities. It took discipline to doubt when you wanted to believe.

By the time my father entered the University of Florida in 1954, the year after Watson and Crick confirmed the helical structure of DNA and free will was overthrown by predetermined encodings, the "softer" sciences had developed "physics envy." The same methods used to observe cells dividing at the other end of a microscope were now applied to observations of animals, including human animals. Behaviorism invaded psychology.

The interiority of the human mind was minimized in relation to exterior and observable data. People were seen as conditioned primarily by their environments; their actions were best understood as responses to external stimuli rather than the deliberate choices of a thinking, feeling self.

If human minds were denied interiority, animals were denied even a mind. Zoology took up the rigors of behaviorism from psychology and condemned "anthropomorphizing," which first meant assuming that animals think and feel the way humans do, but then expanded to mean assuming that animals think and feel at all. At mid-century, animals were simply the manifestations of behaviors and motor patterns.

When he got his PhD in Organic Chemistry in 1962 and began his career developing plastics, my father saw no inconsistency between synthetic polymer experimentation and his interest in wildlife and the natural environment. He loved both science and nature together, and loved them in ways shaped by his culture. He was, in the language of the time, conditioned by his social environment.

By the late 1960s, living in the suburbs, he took my brother and me to the Forest Preserves nearly every weekend the weather permitted. There, armed with butterfly nets and jars stuffed with chloroform-soaked paper towels, we set forth into the wilds. I learned to identify yellow swallowtails and red admirals, and how to distinguish a monarch from a mere viceroy. I also learned that to appreciate nature was to "preserve" it by mounting it in cotton-backed display cases. To love nature was to own it. Nature was something out there, distinct from our human lives; it was something you drive to. It came into the household only through television and *National Geographic* magazines.

Growing up, I tried to be the scientist my father was. I imprinted on him when he modeled rationalism as an instinct, and tried to love the discovery of the natural order as much as he did. I learned to value doubt over belief, and to appreciate how much harder the former is. I learned (though imperfectly) to observe without rushing to interpretation, and to look for the telling detail that would undermine established belief. I took pride, too, in rationalism as an ethic. We didn't fall prey to magical thinking, not even as a comfort for dealing with death.

In my teen years I tried to make my father proud. I studied hard—too hard. I learned to silence my voice, with its many emotions and needs. I stopped wasting time on the fantastical stories and poems I wrote as a child, stopped inhabiting the world of unprovables and impossibilities, and instead adopted the Scientific Method as my worldview. I cultured my skepticism, shunned superstition, and learned how to live without God or afterlife. I learned how to think, really think, without falling into logical fallacies or mistaking links for causes. Order and predictability, I learned, were preferable to transcendent meaning. It was better to be able to calculate your degree of doubt than to believe with all your heart.

"That's all right!" my father said when I won my high school's Bausch & Lomb science award, and "That's not bad!" when I won the CRC freshman chemistry award in college. If I'd maintained a relationship with hidden nuances and irrational meanings, I might have detected the pride and love he was trying to contain with understatement. But I now collected evidence through direct, phenomenological observation, and trusted what could be proven and verified. I was merely "all right" and "okay." I tried harder yet.

Until the day in my junior year of college, where I was majoring in chemistry. I'd begun doing volunteer work in a lab on organometallic compounds and chelating agents, measuring out micrograms of compound too tiny to be seen on the sheet of gold leaf that I could only handle with tweezers because the oils on my fingers would have thrown the weight. Maybe it was the acetone going to my head, or the stuffiness of the un-air-conditioned lab in the middle of Florida, or maybe it was the start of what I would years later recognize as a migraine, but the heavy pressure under my eyes released into tears. It took me a minute to recognize that I was crying. Once I started I couldn't stop. *I hate this*, I said out loud. It took me another minute to recognize hate. It took me a lot longer to figure out what I meant by *this*.

I'm not sure I ever properly analyzed what I hated, what caused me to break down and never enter another lab again. Having trusted in the analytical method for so long and having felt betrayed by it, I reacted by turning as far to the other side as possible. I reacted in hate and haste as I ran to the registrar, dumped all my upper-division science classes for the coming semester (Analytical Chemistry, Biochemistry, Pharmacology), and began again with introductory humanities surveys.

I, too, was very much a woman of my time. I wish I could have recognized then what I see now. Gradually, as classical physics gave way to quantum physics, social science's behaviorism, too, was being challenged. Maybe objectivity and subjectivity were not mutually exclusive. Maybe reason and emotion were not so distinct after all; brain research was showing them to be neurologically related, fraternal if not identical twins.

The gender ideology built into scientific models, too, was being uncovered and subverted. Feminist philosophers and scientists pointed out that, traditionally, the sciences were coded as male, the humanities female—and these two sexes were posed as opposites. The male way of objective, scientific thinking, I'd learned and internalized, was more valuable than the subjective, touchy-feely humanities. But people around me were starting to challenge these traditional attributes, as well as the values we put on them. I wish I'd been one of them. I wish I'd known then how to challenge science's antipathy to "softness" instead of accepting it and then abandoning science altogether.

Had I done so, I would have been ahead of my time. If in earlier eras the "soft" sciences had physics envy, the relationship was now beginning to invert. As faith in the possibility of absolute objectivity waned, subjectivity, or emotional attachment to the subject under study, was slowly becoming a gateway into insight rather than an obstruction of it. The accepted bans on sentiment and anthropomorphism were challenged. The field of Ethology developed to study animals within their habitat rather than, as previously, in labs, where measurements and control groups were possible. "Leakey's Angels"—Jane Goodall, Dian Fossey, and Birutė Galdikas—demonstrated that respect and empathy for other primate species could not only produce unprecedented observational data but also shift the whole paradigm. Charges of anthropomorphism were countered with charges of anthropocentrism—the belief that humans are exceptional and distinct from other animals, particularly in their possession of minds, emotions, and intentions, and, on the collective scale, of language and culture. Maybe the model of strict objectivity was itself biased and obscuring, according to these new ethologists. Debates were rekindled: Do animals have emotions? Do they have psyches? Do they have culture? Can they love, or yearn, or grieve? Do they have emotions we don't even know how to recognize or name? This new wave of ethology is summed up in animal ethologist Frans de Waal's oft-cited assertion, "To endow animals with human emotions has long been a scientific taboo. But if we do not, we risk missing something fundamental, about both animals and us."

We are now working to recover that fundamental something that we've missed.

Still, the anti-sentimental bias is alive and well today, even in the humanities, including creative writing. Good, strong, muscular writing—hard writing—is without soft sentiment. Stoic observation is preferred over—and is seen as the opposite of—emoting. A writing professor once explained to me that, rather than allowing my characters to cry, I should show them holding back tears; the latter act is much more "powerful." The anti-sentimental bias culminates in the "show, don't tell" mandate, creative writing's analog to the scientific method.

My father lived the "show, don't tell" ethos. I don't remember his ever saying *I love you*. Instead, he showed it. He took me to the Forest Preserves weekly and museums monthly, helped me with years of homework, drove me to tennis matches, and, later, read every essay I produced as a fledgling writer. ("That's all right!" he'd comment when he was feeling especially verbose.) He was a scientist to the end, and he trusted that deeds speak louder than words. But sometimes the facts *don't* speak for themselves.

My father died of a stroke in 1995. I was already an adult and had been living away from home for years, with a PhD in English literature and a university teaching position. He never had told me he loved me, but I had just begun hearing it anyway, if only faintly and from afar. I returned to Florida for the unsentimental Jewish funeral my mother gave him, as he would have wanted. It wasn't until I went out walking for air and literally stumbled over a plaintively meowing stray cat, who wouldn't leave my ankles, that I was able to wail. Even then, I felt the pull of rationality's moral imperative not to read anything mystic or superstitious into this eerily orange *felis catus* appearing insistently from out of nowhere, pushing its facial scent glands into my shins, butting its head under my palms, tempting me with meaning.

Recently, on the anniversary of my father's death—what Jews call the *yahrzeit*, Yiddish for year-time—I searched for a way to mark it. Estranged from the Judaism I was raised with, in part because of the rationalism I was also reared in, I still light a yahrzeit candle every year, but as always it seemed inadequate. Without the framework of a formal religion, I've had to invent my own rituals, going only by feel and instinct. Then I remembered our *Wild Kingdom* ritual. For lack of any better way to mourn my father or memorialize the event, I turned on the TV to Animal Planet, which I'd heard had recently revived *Mutual of Omaha's Wild Kingdom*, half hoping to be greeted by white-haired Marlin Perkins himself, even though he died two decades ago. It would be hard, but I would force myself to watch nature's ravages.

Instead I landed on a show called *Big Cat Diary*, which follows three young mothers—a cheetah, a leopard, and a lioness—as they attempt to keep their cubs (called "pups") alive in unforgiving African terrain. Tamu, the lioness, was struggling the hardest, because she'd been expelled from the pride headed by the lion who impregnated her, and was on her own with her four pups. Then she was attacked by a young male lion, who wanted to kill her pups so that, as the tracker explained, she would come into heat faster and then he could impregnate her with his own genetic pool. (That's my recollection; I'm sure his wording was much less anthropomorphic and more behaviorist.) After the attack, only two pups were left. One had been badly injured, but limped away with his mama and brother to safety. Tamu went back for the missing pups but couldn't find them, and when she returned to the surviving pups, the injured one had died.

"Oh no," said the tracker, who doubled as narrator, a white man with a British accent contrasting with the voices of the African sorrow song that came in lightly as soundtrack. "Oh no, oh no, oh no." He was tearing up, in danger of spilling, and clearly embarrassed as a man and a scientist, so he took cover behind his binoculars. We watched with him as Tamu leant over the dead pup, and then began to lick it with a tongue almost as wide as its small corpse. Her motions were those of a mother licking the amniotic fluid off a newborn, licking him into life. "Is she confused?" the Brit said in voice-over. "Does she not realize he's dead? Or is it ... I hesitate to say that this is an expression of caring."

My father would have hesitated, too, and perhaps I should have done so in honor of his memory. But as a failed scientist, I can unapologetically say what scientists can't, what I know to be true even if it's not verifiable: Tamu was grieving. Nothing could be clearer. As her surviving pup sniffed at the corpse and bit at Tamu's leg, she felt with her muscular tongue the last warmth of her child's body.

In some ways, I am my father's daughter after all. Since that yahrzeit viewing, I've become addicted to Animal Planet. It's now my soap opera. I take my vegetarian dinners in front of the TV and rail at the untold cruelties of nature while the big cats face their mortality with dignity.

Later in that yahrzeit episode, Tamu went back yet again to the site of the attack where she lost her other two pups. "She just can't let go," said the Brit sadly. He disapproved of her risk, leaving her one surviving pup alone to go after two pups who couldn't possibly be alive two-and-a-half days later.

"But what's that?" he said, with three glottal stops. "Hell-oo?" Emerging out of the tall grass were three figures—Tamu and her two starving pups, alive with yelps of hunger. "Good girl, Tamu!" gushed the Brit. He couldn't help himself. "Incredible! What joy!" He was tearing up, with happiness this time, clearly ashamed of himself, but unable to contain his instinct to anthropomorphize. Trying to recover his composure, he summed up, "And now we go on, and try to keep the three remaining pups alive."

And now we go on. But I'm still lingering over the dead pup. At this time of yahrzeit, the scene of mourning that my juvenile self learned to rationalize and repress now haunts me. I replay it in slow motion on the screen behind my eyes: the image of Tamu's maternal tongue, muscular and soft, searching the surface of the pup's body, burying it in licks and breath and silence.

3/ The Meaning of Meat

Cat. *noun.* a small, domesticated carnivore.

Sunday was hamburger night: charred patties in fat-absorbing white buns with ketchup, mustard, and piccalilli. Five decades ago, back when my age could still be written in single digits, the highlight of the week was *Mutual of Omaha's Wild Kingdom.* My father and I got to eat our Sunday dinner on TV trays set up in the den. We'd turn the ketchup bottle upside down as we heard the Mutual of Omaha jingle so that by the time the show started it would pour out in perfect blood-red splotches.

Because of my brother's allergies, we couldn't keep free-ranging pets in the house, so my knowledge of animal life came largely from my caged hamsters and from *Mutual of Omaha's Wild Kingdom.* (We always said the full title, all five words.) I liked the mammals best, especially the tree-climbing herbivores, but my father was most fascinated by the reptiles and amphibians, and, of course, the big cats. I loved to watch my father, his blue eyes flickering with the television light, as he watched the animals. He came alive, adding details to Marlin Perkins': a rustle of leaves where hidden presences lurked; the way the lioness pulled back her lips to smell through her mouth. So as not to sabotage our time together, I feigned fascination too, and never told him about my recurring nightmares: the lioness's jaw closing around my neck; the alligators creeping out from under my bed to eat me alive; the bear that hibernated in the closet emerging in the dark and tearing off my face with a single swipe.

Nor did I tell my dad how, awake and going about my day, I felt the eyes of a panther on me, assessing me for the pounce.

It wasn't so much fear of being eaten that really traumatized me, though. It was the whole system. Nature was crueler and more heartless than I could handle. My father explained to me that every living thing on earth must eventually die, and many creatures would die at the hands of another. What I saw as murder was natural, necessary, and normal. "If you can't accept that, you're going to have a tough time," my father laughed. Watching *Mutual of Omaha's Wild Kingdom*, I decided that there couldn't be a God behind all this, or how would He choose between the starving cheetah and the flailing antelope?

Yet my tender-heartedness never translated into self-awareness. Although we must have eaten several hundred hamburgers over those many years in front of the TV on Sunday evenings, back when we thought it healthy to eat red meat, I never recognized myself as a predator, or the meat on my plate as a kill.

Twenty years later, I was still a meat-eater. I had not become a scientist like my father but was attending graduate school in Houston for English literature. I was living with a group of Indian men: Rajiv, who would become my life-partner, and his two Bengali friends. I was the only female, the only Caucasian, and the only American in the household, so I did a lot of cultural translating. When Thanksgiving came around, I don't think my Indian roommates quite understood its import beyond the bestowal of a four-day weekend. My explanation—that the pilgrims gave thanks to their God as a kind of Christian adaptation of sacrificial animal offerings to pagan deities—probably didn't help. My roommates, meat-eating Hindus, proposed a cookout on the balcony of our second-floor apartment. The clouds gathered as Ranabir lit the grill, and the first drops fell as Dipankar put on the glistening chicken. Rajiv, a doctoral student in engineering, rigged up a canopy from sheets and twine, and we lounged under it as the rain bounced off the fabric, its splat sounds blending with the spitting and crackling of chicken fat.

The little gray cat must have smelled the charring flesh too, and must have been near starvation to brave the balcony stairs and the presence of humans. Scrawny and semi-feral, she bore deep green eyes that dominated her silvery face. She scattered at our every move but kept returning. We modulated our movements to tai chi slowness, encouraged her with falsetto coos, and gave her the first breast, cut into chunks and offered on a paper plate. She snatched a bit and darted away, but the taste of meat in her mouth emboldened her, and she returned to devour it, watching us with wide and wary eyes.

Over the next few days she reappeared and was given tuna fish. I bought some cans of cat food, which she took in a bowl out on the porch. One cold night she ventured into the house and slept behind the sofa. We'd been calling her Kitty for weeks before we realized that she was our cat now, and the name stuck. When Ranu and Dipu moved out, Rajiv and I set up a blanket and litter box for her in the extra bedroom.

Then Kitty began leaving us "presents"—mostly mice and birds, ripped open but barely eaten, laid out on our welcome mat. She seemed appalled at our responses to those gifts—my shrieks and Rajiv's hasty disposal of them—and I felt her haughty condescension at our inability to appreciate the import of the kill. For my part, I had trouble reconciling this beautiful, silvery cat, who nestled in Rajiv's crotch while he worked at the computer, with the heartless psychopath who killed not for sustenance but for sport—for the *joy* of it. "The opposite of a psychopath is an empath," Rajiv laughed, his sharp Adam's apple bobbing. "And both are pathological." Then he added, as my father had years earlier, "If you're this tender-hearted, how are you ever going to survive?"

Kitty's impulse was as old as the domestication of cats. The first wildcat may have ventured into human presence in the Near East's Fertile Crescent around ten thousand years ago, when nomadic tribes began to exchange a hunter-gatherer lifestyle for one of agriculture, and their diet changed from primarily meat-based to primarily grain-based. Not half a step behind the shift to grain production and storage was an influx of opportunistic rodents, and, just behind them, predatory wildcats. As carnivores, cats didn't eat the rye, wheat, oats, or barley, but homed in on the scuttling meat that these grains attracted. Cats were domesticated—or domesticated themselves—as hunters and meat-eaters. That was their niche, their job, and their identity. Nothing could be more natural.

From these early wildcats arose our housecat. A recent excavation in Cyprus, dated at 9,500 years ago, revealed the body of a young cat buried with a human. Human lives—and deaths—have been intimately bound together with those of cats for at least as long as these two skeletons lay wrapped around each other.

In ancient Egyptian culture and elsewhere, cats rose to demi-god status, so important were they to the economy. Taken aboard ships to quell the rodent population, domestic cats quickly spread throughout the Roman Empire and beyond. Ironically, it was cats' carnivorousness that enabled humans to eat a grain-based diet, which in turn helped humans to spread their dominion across the earth.

At times, the cat's importance to agriculture was recognized, and the cat was revered, idolized, even deified. Mohammed's adoration of his cat is legendary, and the Norse goddess of fertility, Freyja, was frequently depicted in a chariot drawn by cats. By the time Christianity spread throughout Europe and beyond, cats had a cult-like status as pagan symbols of fertility and plentitude. This cat-worship threatened the new regime, which began to associate cats with both paganism and the devil. They became witches' familiars, harbingers of bad luck, even succubae who stole good Christians' souls. Such medieval superstitions led to massive cat-killings. Scholars today believe that the Black Plague of the mid-fourteenth century reached the epidemic proportions that it did because mass cat-killings had allowed the rat population to flourish.

Like those cats among the ancient Egyptians, Kitty domesticated herself into the lives of Rajiv and me. For years, it was the three of us. Even though she was only eight pounds at her heaviest, Kitty seemed to fill the household. She held her own as a family member, and more than earned her keep as a mouser.

If we'd never rented that video on cats from the library, we would even have thought she loved us. Her head-butts and cheek-rubbings expressed affection, we thought—until we learned that she was rubbing her scent glands onto us to mark us as her property. (Or maybe that's what love *is*.) Except for the deception of size, the video told us, cats' bodies are remarkably similar in form and function to the massive felines of the jungles and forests. Kitty's paws, usually so soft, could become instant switchblades if she let loose her retracted claws. Her fang teeth were perfectly positioned to break the spine of her prey, while her smaller front teeth excelled at the delicate work of stripping fur and feathers.

Kitty purred in Rajiv's lap as we watched the video with increasing dismay. "She's a killing machine," Rajiv said. I thought I detected, amidst the horror in his voice, just a touch of awe.

The triglycerides in a meat-based diet are rich in saturated fats, which are known to accumulate in arteries, molecule by molecule, year by year, until one day an artery becomes completely blocked.

When my father died of a stroke, in 1995, my mother gave him an unsentimental Jewish funeral, which he would have wanted, but which left me, still in shock's sedation, unmoved. The stone cemetery marker, already in place and engraved, seemed eternal, its precisely etched birth and death dates making his end seem pre-determined. The solidity of that headstone, the right angles of the thick pine coffin: I couldn't reconcile them with my urgent sense of fragility, of injustice, of downright incredulity.

After the short ceremony and the Kaddish, after we each dropped a handful of dirt into the grave, I lingered to watch the workers' more efficient shoveling until Rajiv led me out of the cemetery grounds. Once past the gates, he confessed that all those rotting, insect-preyed bodies underground made him queasy. Raised with cremation, he found our Western attachment to the body alien and a bit barbaric. Numbly, I promised to cremate him, and made him do the same for me if I went first. But nothing really registered. Our deaths were as unreal as my father's.

It wasn't until we rounded the corner past the cemetery gates, and I felt the shadow of a brush at my ankles, that my face twitched. When I bent down to pet the mewing cat, my mask melted. The cat mewed and mewed, trebling my wails.

"Maybe the cat is a sign," Rajiv said. "Maybe it's trying to tell us something."

I wanted him to be right. But my father, a scientist through and through, wouldn't give me a sign; he taught me not to believe in signs, or in an afterlife, or even in souls separable from bodies. Every living thing dies, and all you can do is accept it. Or struggle.

Over the years, as Rajiv and I pursued our careers—he an environmental engineering professor, I an English professor—we moved Kitty from place to place, finally landing in Colorado. Once settled and with a backyard, we began accumulating additional animals, including two more cats and three dogs. But, aside from the unresponsive hamsters and gerbils I kept as a child, Kitty would always be my first. Her presence in our lives was almost as old as our love for each other, and equally as abiding, reliable, and at times ferocious.

A bit of the feral always remained in Kitty. We could be petting her for a good ten minutes, her eyes closed and motor running, when, suddenly deciding she'd had enough, she'd hiss and scratch at us until we recoiled. "That's our Kitty," Rajiv would laugh, and try to scratch her between the ears, provoking another swipe.

As the three of us stalked middle age, Kitty's carnal gifts slowed and then stopped. She spent more time in the house, curled up in our garage-sale papasan. She became, at last, a pet.

Pets are supposed to die before their owners. Rajiv's diagnosis of Stage IV (metastatic, terminal) colon cancer at age thirty-seven made no sense.

It ruptured reality. Time froze in that waiting room in the hospital basement with nothing to read but *Field & Stream*: Rajiv emerging with a "thumbs down," the doctor following with the glossy photo of the anemone-like tumor among sea-form polyps. My legs trembling. Rajiv helping me off the floor, where a part of me remains.

Then time raced. It all went so quickly: our first twelve years together, the diagnosis, the eleven months of chemo and radiation and palliative surgeries, the liver failure, the dying, the death in the middle of the night, the disappearance of Rajiv's body into the funeral home's oversized station wagon, the cremation.

Kitty had continued to sleep on Rajiv's stomach until his swollen liver couldn't bear her weight on his ribcage anymore.

I've tried to resist superstition and magical thinking in my attempts to make sense of Rajiv's senseless death. After all, Rajiv, like my father, was a scientist. But everything around me seemed to be a sign.

Two mornings after he died, when I was still in cocooned in shock's unreality, I left to make arrangements at the funeral home. I got as far as the garage and screamed. On top of Rajiv's car was some sort of bloody atrocity, which, as I stepped closer, resolved itself into an eviscerated squirrel. I gagged, then sobbed. Surely this was Kitty's doing. What was she thinking?

Then I realized that I had to dispose of the body, which was supposed to be Rajiv's job, which triggered a fresh wave of sobs, which mercifully blurred my vision of the carcass. This would be my first body—to be quickly followed, I realized ironically, by Rajiv's—that I would have to dispose of myself. I pulled myself together enough to prepare a black plastic garbage bag, the heavy-duty kind for garden work, took a deep breath, and climbed onto the hood of the car.

The squirrel, its tiny mouth open as if gasping, was arranged in a cross, belly-up to display Kitty's perfect visceral extraction. The sacrificial pose was too symmetrical to be arbitrary. This body was carefully arranged. I couldn't look to see how much of the guts were left, but the rest of the body was still intact. The placement and shape of this offering, unlike previous ones, was deliberate, intentional even. I tried to picture Kitty pulling the heavy squirrel carcass, gripped between her teeth, up onto the car's hood, then higher up to its top, and then arranging it precisely.

As I eased the stiff carcass into its body bag, I chanted, "I'm sorry, squirrel. I'm so sorry. It's not fair. It's not okay. It's not acceptable. It's just not." I knew the squirrel couldn't hear me—that it was well into rigor mortis, and that anyway it was a squirrel—but this needless, merciless, senseless death demanded an apology. At the same time, I couldn't help being a little in awe of Kitty's act, couldn't resist seeing it as a crude sacrifice and primal mourning ritual.

Among humans, death seems to demand a sacrifice. Ensconced in grief, I became fascinated with the mourning practices of different cultures. Sacrifice, I found, is a way of "making sacred." The transformation of flesh into smoke and ashes symbolizes the movement of physical being to spirit. It was also, for pre-modern societies, a way to keep the dead body from attracting predators. But sometimes it was not only the person being mourned who was burned. Many traditions have killed and burned other animals, even human animals, in the mourning ceremony. Famously, after Achilles' beloved Patroclus was killed in combat in the Trojan War, as Homer recounts it in his *Iliad*, Achilles went on an orgy of sacrifice, adding horses, dogs, and twelve captive Trojan men to Patroclus' funeral pyre.

The eating of the bodies burned, particularly in animal sacrifice, is a central part of many ritual sacrifices—so much so that one anthropological theory has animal sacrifice arising from guilt over meat-eating. The animal killed and consumed was, at the same time, thanked and mourned. Ancient Greek civilizations, for one, seem to have had deep, irreconcilable ambivalences over the killing of other animals, over making others die so that they may live. Ritual sacrifice was a kind of "compromise formation" to reconcile butchery with that nebulous entity called guilt, or conscience, or the gods.

Humans are said to be the only animals who perform rituals and sacrifices. But Kitty's offering makes me wonder.

Sacrifice is not an option for me. I have no gods to thank for my meat, but only guilt and excessive empathy, which can never be appeased. After Rajiv's death, I started taking vegetarianism seriously. I'd been leaning towards it for a long time. Guilt over the treatment of animals at factory farms was a big factor. Rajiv's research in groundwater contamination had led him to investigate cows' elimination of over-injected antibiotics, which wound their way into soil, rivers, and fish. A clandestine field trip with him to a local McFarm in Northern Colorado horrified me: cows lined up in stalls ass to ass and wading in their own and others' excrement. Rajiv's environmentalism also led us to the realization that meat-eating is not sustainable, and is both depleting and warming our environment at an unconscionable rate. I also, after Rajiv's death, turned to vegetarianism as a tribute to his Hinduism, though he, himself, violated its dietary philosophies. Beyond principles, though, I was still the little girl unable to handle death, even on television or off-stage. If I were honest, I would have to admit that I was primarily motivated in my vegetarianism not by any of the noble factors I regularly listed to people, but by the ick factor.

The smell of burning flesh as we shoved Rajiv's body into the incinerator: this is almost surely a false memory, but it's as distinct and vivid as any memory I possess. I recall the shock at the recognition of the smell of meat on the grill. Although the flash of recognition almost surely didn't happen the way I replay it mentally, its reverse is a regular occurrence: the smell of cooked meat, the flash of recognition that meat is a dead body.

But I am a hypocrite. Even though I've been meatless long enough that meat has begun to disgust me, even though I've recharted my path through the grocery store to avoid the butchery and the carnage of luncheon meat, even though I once gagged on the moving walkway of the airport as it passed a restaurant advertisement featuring a money-shot photo of a plate of brisket, I still feed meat to my animals. It's conveniently disguised as kibble, arriving in little pellets far removed from the suggestion of animal carcasses, though I still have to hold my breath as I scoop it into bowls. I tell myself that cats are "obligate carnivores"; they must eat meat. It's their nature. Dogs don't require meat, and a careful vegetarian can satisfy a dog's nutritional needs with balanced portions of beans and whole grains. But my dogs disdain my carrots and leftover lentil beans, while meat is a magnet. Only meat will work as training bits. A dog's attraction to meat is far beyond, or far before, hunger or need. It's absolutely real, and absolutely animal. It demands respect.

I still understand the call of meat—the way the imperative to consume animal protein *feels* absolutely natural, whether it is or not. Once in a while, when I'm really hungry and premenstrual and my amino acid balance is off along with my electrolytes, something primal takes over. I flip from my usual mode of pathological empathy to the carnivorousness of the big cat on the African savannah. Once when I got home late and had hardly eaten all day, I quickly fed the critters before feeding myself. As I was spooning out Kitty's wet food from a can, my nose caught a whiff of the mushy mass in reddish-brown gravy. I found myself salivating so effusively I had to suck up a strand of drool before it hit Kitty's bowl.

I'd switched Kitty to wet food when her decline in health made her finicky. At age seventeen, four years after Rajiv's death, she developed mammary gland cancer, and quickly her chest was studded with hard lumps. The university vet school recommended chemo, surgery, and radiation, but I declined. Rajiv had chosen these tortuous treatments, but imposing them on a geriatric cat without choice or understanding was simply torture. Selfishly, too, I knew I couldn't go through that kind of caregiving again, not even with a cat. Rajiv's suffering and death nearly killed me.

Miraculously, Kitty lived on for two more years, her svelte eight pounds dipping to a dangerous six. I gave her all the wet food she wanted, in increasingly complex gourmet flavors and textures. She had "medleys" and "casseroles" of "minced," "flaked," "marinated," "roasted," and "grilled" meats, all in "rich gravies" and "bisques" and "stews." Kitty greeted me each morning with her customary quack, demanding food. Throughout the day more quacking, more eating. She fed the tumors—

one the size of an apricot, others like full-season cherries, bunched like the cluster of varicose veins that once hung on my father's thigh.

As she declined, Kitty developed the telltale old cat smell, fishy and slightly rancid. She squawked at me as I tried to comb the mats out of the fur that she used to groom so punctiliously, now thick with oils, dander, dust, and decay. She squawked when I stopped brushing. She squawked when I resumed. Unable to find comfort, she quacked for more food.

When the quacking stopped I knew we were nearing the end.

As the vet had predicted, Kitty tried to go away to die. She stumbled around the back yard between bouts of collapse. At one point she hobbled up on her failing hips and walked over to the Buddha statue I'd gotten because his broad nose and high cheekbones reminded me of Rajiv's. Fresh rain had pooled in the Buddha's cupped hands. Kitty took one lap, then another, then, miraculously another, before flopping back into a deep sleep. Next time I checked on her, she had a huge splotch of bird poop on her fur that she hadn't bothered to clean up. She tried to hiss when I cleaned it off her. With her mouth wide open, bobbing for oxygen, her breathing looked just like vomiting. One eye was dripping goop. The other looked pleading. It was time.

But on the veterinary table, catheter in her leg, Kitty seemed to rally. The vet gave us a few last minutes alone together. Kitty poked her head up, then stood up on her arthritic legs, and walked around the examining table. She seemed curious, or maybe there was still some fight in her. Was I wrong?

"Quick, wrap her in the towel and make a run for it," a familiar voice said in my head. It was Rajiv's. I shook with a laugh that produced tears.

The procedure was quick. It was nothing like Rajiv's death of labor and strain to the end, each breath struggling to pull yet one more after it. His agony seemed so unnatural, so cosmically wrong, that I'll never be OK with it. But Kitty's artificial death seemed much more natural. The vet injected the medicine and Kitty's head settled into her front paws. By the time the injection was completed Kitty was dead. In those few moments after she drew her last breath and before she began to stiffen, she looked more alive than when she was dying. Her eyes, which hadn't been truly open for ages, were wide with green memories.

I remembered her squirrel sacrifice. Kitty deserved to have her death marked dramatically, performed in wild style, with ritual cruelty. But in spite of her life of flaming carnivorousness, I merely had her cremated, and poured her ashes into the Big Thompson River in Rocky Mountain National Park, where they would follow Rajiv's. Both bodies returned to the ecosystem and the cycle of life without ever becoming meat.

I still can't accept this cycle of life, or the necessity of death. If my veg-etarianism is merely an attempt to live in denial of the unacceptable, so be it. Meat is natural, my carnivorous friends tell me, whereas empathy for prey goes against nature.

Well, the truth is that I *am* against nature. I can't stomach it. If meat is natural then death is natural, and to eat meat is to be OK with death.

As my father and Rajiv had both warned me, that level of tender-hearted denial of reality makes for a tough time. Resisting the natural-ness of death is a fight that can never be won.

I read recently that if a person dies in her home, the cats will start eating her body in less than twenty-four hours, whereas the dogs will wait over a day before partaking. The odds are good that I will die in my home, in the presence of my remaining dogs and cats, with no other humans around. I wonder if the canines would fend off the felines for a while, or stand by as my cats, unfed and hungry, begin to nibble. I can picture the three spaniels bent over me with ears flopping forward, wait-ing for alpha Olive, my bossy border collie, to stop nipping and butting at my shins, trying to nose me back into life. She will then give them the signal to begin, and they'll each grab a limb, while the cats go for the gut. It might take a while for the human world to miss me; by the time humans come for my body the animals will be close to the bone.

Despite my tender-heartedness, I am at peace with this vision. More than that: I hope they will experience in this act, if not love, then communion, or even the orgiastic ecstasy of ancient sacrifice rituals, where one symbolically, or literally, eats one's elders to incorporate them into one's own body. Maybe their feeding will make me sacred, or at least carry me on in their animal bodies. If so, I hope that there's a rush of nourishment when my domesticated beasts finally, for perhaps the first time in their lives, taste real meat: raw, fresh, fleshy, bloody, and absolutely natural.

4/ The Blue Heron Returns

"And have you had a visit from your husband since he died?" Marilyn asks me this at the gym, on the recovery station between reps, after I divulge to my new acquaintance that I'm a widow. People generally respond to my story by anxiously trying to comfort me, quickly asserting that Rajiv isn't really dead, or that he's in heaven, or that he lives on in memory. But most don't come right out and assert, as Marilyn does, that he walks the earth in some ghostly dimension. She tells me she can feel his presence right there by my side, one step behind me on the exercise mat.

I smile politely, but remain stubbornly uncomforted. I can't believe in ghosts. As an atheist, and in allegiance to Rajiv, it's been a moral imperative for me, and perhaps a secret source of pride, to live without magic and to refuse metaphysical anodynes. So I don't tell Marilyn about my blue heron.

*

Aunt Eleanor, my mother's older sister, flew in from Miami Beach to see Rajiv one last time before he died. Rajiv, my life partner of thirteen years, was nearing the end-stage of metastatic colon cancer. Aunt Eleanor's husband, my Uncle Bob, had died fourteen years earlier of complications from colon cancer. Bob used to appear to her in the form of a stray cat on her porch, or so she believed. She fed him chicken strips and tuna fish. When the cat appeared on the porch my cousin Mark would call out, "Mom, your husband's hungry."

So now I asked Aunt Eleanor if she still fed the stray cat. "No, no cats come around any more. I'm starting to think that that cat never was Bob after all." She speaks in warm, tragic-comic, Jewish-New Jersey cadences. "I think it was birds all along."

"Birds?" I didn't know if I was teasing her or not.

"This one bird sings right outside my window. I think it's Bob. I do. Bob always liked to sing. He had a wonderful voice. Even after he got the cancer he played Buffalo Bill in *Annie Get Your Gun* over at the community theater. He sang to me as I left for this trip. He sang, 'Goodbye, have a good trip.'"

I glanced at Rajiv and he glanced at me. We smiled.

Aunt Eleanor called when she got back to Miami Beach. "I saw Bob in the airport!" she gushed. "I did. I saw Bob in the Denver airport. There was a bird flying around in the Denver airport, and he looked right at me. He did. Who ever heard of a bird in an airport? It had to be Bob, taking me back home, telling me everything would be okay."

I didn't have the heart to tell her that I've been seeing birds in the big white parachute of an airport since my first landing there for my job interview.

When I reported Aunt Eleanor's phone conversation, Rajiv and I had a good laugh over it. Although he was raised Hindu, he had no faith whatsoever in reincarnation. "Will you come back to me as a bird?" I teased.

"Sure," he laughed, but this time without smiling. "I'll come back and visit you as a bird. What sort of fowl would you like?"

"Anything but a turkey." Or a vulture, I didn't add.

*

Rajiv was diagnosed with colon cancer on Thursday, July 12. The next day the liver scan and biopsy delivered his death sentence: metastases in all four quadrants of the liver meant—Rajiv asked the oncologist to tell him bluntly—that he had six months without treatment, a bit longer with treatment—if it worked. After the oncologist came and went, after I cried so violently that a nurse named Candy offered me a sedative, after Rajiv circled me in his arms as if I were the sick one and warned me not to dehydrate myself, after I ran dry, I noted that it was Friday the thirteenth. "No," Rajiv said simply. "We're not going to fly off into the realm of superstition and magic." Schooled in engineering, he was a true scientist at heart. His rationality anchored my instinct for air.

Though raised in India, Rajiv put his faith in Western medicine and faced his treatment squarely. But the chemo drugs didn't work much better than hope or prayer or the sheer unrelenting will to live. In the parlance of the oncologist, Rajiv "failed." In the middle of the night on June 2, three days after his thirty-eighth birthday, under eleven months after his diagnosis, and after hours of straining for breath, his face relaxed, and he became an inert thing.

One moment he was alive and grasping, the next he was dead. It was inconceivable, unthinkable, as if all the known laws of physics had been suspended.

*

Driving Marge home from our grief support group, I asked her about the peacock pin she wore on the left front pocket of her oversized jean jacket. I couldn't tell whether the peacock was silver or gold under the iridescent pinks, greens, purples, and blues of its many-eyed feathers.

"Didn't I tell you about the peacocks and nails that day I met you in the towel aisle at Target?"

I shook my head. (I'd been finding myself wandering towel and curtain aisles, needing to touch every fabric. Something of promise in the bright, tactile colors. "Sexture," Rajiv had called such butter-smooth material.)

"Well, Dan was a carpenter," Marge reminded me, fishing around in her oversized pocket. "He loved to build things. He built our house. After he died he left me nails." She pulled out a sample, held it out for me to touch. "Everywhere. I'd find them in all kinds of places they never should have been: among the silverware, under the bed, in my underwear drawer. There's no other way to explain how they got there. It was Dan, giving me signs." Marge put the nail back in her pocket. "I don't find nails so much anymore, but Dan still leaves them for me every once in a while."

"I'm glad for you." And maybe a little jealous, too. I pointed to the pin. "And the peacocks?"

Marge pulled at a cuticle on her ring finger. "When I started dating Mark I asked him about his wife, who'd died around the time Dan did. I met Mark in another grief support group, you know, at my church? Have you met Mark? Of course—that was him with me in Target. This is his jacket." Marge stopped pulling at the cuticle—it was bleeding now—and began to finger the pin without unclasping it from the jacket. "Mark and I talk about our spouses all the time. I like hearing him talk about his wife. So one day we were driving in the car and Mark mentioned that his wife liked peacocks. Then, not an hour later, I swear it, we saw a metal peacock lawn ornament on someone's front yard. You see flamingoes all the time, but never peacocks. We'd been on our way to a flea market. When we walked into the store, there, right at the door, in the glass display case, was this peacock pin. Now we see peacocks all the time. It's Mark's wife, I know it is." Marge patted the pin back into the denim. "Mark doesn't believe it. But I do. So I wear this peacock in her honor. And a nail in my pocket."

*

I searched the grief books that friends kindly brought to me in the days and weeks after Rajiv's death, but I found no mention of this phenomenon, although it's common among the bereaved. Everyone in my grief support group had a sign. Bereft, we fall into a kaleidoscope of colors and shapes without meaning—and then suddenly there's meaning where none was expected. The physical world becomes a language of signs, and grief the translator. We read the signs.

There must be mention of these phenomena somewhere—some validation of them, or refutation, some acknowledgement or warning—but they appeared nowhere in the common grief books of the self-help ilk. There was mention of faith, mostly (implicitly) of Christian faith: the power of faith as a sustainer; the crisis of faith that often occurs in a griever whose faith has always been rock-solid; the turning to faith in a griever previously uninterested in religion. Those institutionalized expressions of faith are validated, but not these idiosyncratic acts of a spontaneous personal faith, these makeshift metaphysics. The wolf that stared at Steve from behind his barn the first morning after his wife died. The favorite picture that shook so hard in Nikki's bathroom that she had to tell her dead husband to stop it, he was scaring her. The unknown fox that pauses in its creeping.

*

Two days after Rajiv died, a tremendous bird, gray and shimmering, landed on our backyard fence and perched for over an hour, staring at me unblinkingly as I blinked back at him from the bedroom window. He was astonishing, not just in his size but in his *presence*, and in his disproportion with my suburban backyard. A seemingly fantastic creature, prehistoric and eternal, almost—did I dare?—otherworldly. I watched and waited. Then slowly I went downstairs to tell Rajiv's mother. "That is Rajiv," she said with her serene Hindu conviction. We watched from the kitchen window for some time, and then Ma told me I should give the bird some food. But when I brought out a bowl of rice he flew away.

Illiterate in ornithology, I studied the photos that came up on internet searches until I assured myself that it was the Great Blue Heron. The website said that the natural habitat of this wading bird was the Southern swamplands, where it fed on fish, but that it did appear in wetlands in the West and throughout North America. A migratory bird, it materialized near bodies of water—which my scorched suburban Colorado backyard did not provide. Before I could stop myself, I matched fact with fact. A true Bengali, Rajiv did love his fish. His environmental engineering research was in cleanup of groundwater contamination, and particularly of leakage from munitions factories into swampland. He'd even done fieldwork in knee-high rubber boots in the swamps of Tennessee. What better avatar to assume if he wanted to give me a sign?

*

I am rational, I reminded myself. I do not believe in magic, nor do I let myself indulge in magical thinking. I know how to explain these sightings, these signs of return. Although the grief books don't talk about returnings, they do talk, and at length, about the loss of coherence the griever undergoes. Amidst too many bashings of Elizabeth Kübler-Ross's five-stage model of grief, these books offer corrective models. Most include a phase in which the griever acknowledges the reality of the death; a phase in which the reality of death then seems to conflict with the griever's previous beliefs about the way the world is supposed to work, so that the only reality is, temporarily, the reality of death; and a phase of reclamation and rebuilding, in which the griever erects new or strengthened beliefs about the way the world works. As humans, we structure our world to make sense, to explain it to ourselves. With the loss of the center of our lives, that structure tumbles. I know this. What's called "grief work" is, in part, the work of reconstructing our structures of meaning, often in new patterns. But the books don't talk about meaningfulness during the grief work. They talk about the sense of meaninglessness between two coherent systems of meaning, but not the rushes of uncanny recognition.

We grievers, though, know more. We know that in that liminal space anything can happen. Signs slip out of the hands of their assigned meanings and fall into other hands. We become hyper-sensitized to the stimuli around us. We are easily overwhelmed. Significance bounces off the wall and rebounds to the other side. Everything is potentially meaningful. Indistinct clouds metamorphose into fantastic shapes: peacocks, herons, ladybugs.

*

Ladybug, Ladybug, fly away home.
Your house is on fire, your children are gone.

Cindy, a member of my grief-writing group, invoked Jesus with an insistence that disturbed me. Her teenaged daughter died of ecstasy; she'd mixed X with alcohol, collapsed from hypothermia, and died after a three-day coma. Cindy clung doggedly to God. Her powerful prose pieces were always sandwiched by praises to Jesus. The praises were trite and formulaic, but in the body her anger nearly burst out of its skin before being quickly, anxiously submerged again. Cindy did not like it when anyone deviated from Christian belief. She gave no verbal support (as we all always did for each other) when Katie tearfully read her piece about having doubts that prayer does any good, that God even listens. When Rhonda, our facilitator, prompted us to write a poem in which we ask questions twice and answer them in two different ways, explaining that "there can be many truths, not just one," Cindy mumbled under her breath "There is ONE truth."

Then Rhonda had us write concrete poems in shapes of our own choosing, with a circle as example. Mine followed the path in Rocky Mountain National Park along which Rajiv's ashes must have flowed. Cindy drew a ladybug, then wrote words around it, phrases like "You're in Jesus' arms now" and "We will meet again in heaven." Rhonda asked, why a ladybug?

"Because Jenny comes to me as a ladybug. I see ladybugs all the time now. That's Jenny telling me she's with me." Cindy recited this information with less inflection than one does when announcing one's name to the doctor's front office receptionist. It was just a fact.

I asked my friend Kelley, an expert on all things Christian, if ladybug returns were consistent with Cindy's strict Christianity. "The Bible tells us that we're not supposed to try to communicate with the dead," he pronounced decisively before faltering. "... But then, there was the case of Lazarus..."

"So is it blasphemy or not? Is it kosher? Do you believe it?"

"I don't know. Sorry. There are things we just don't know."

Things that aren't in the book.

*

Seven days after Rajiv died, as I tried to weed the menacing tentacles appearing overnight in the new garden Rajiv had planted in his last days, another blue heron landed. This one wasn't as big as the first, but still glorious. He lurked on the roof next door, his shoulders hunched and head thrust forward the way Rajiv's did in the cold, and just looked down at the dogs and me for a while, head-crest flicking from time to time, until my dog Chappy, raising his nose like a weathervane, caught first scent, then sight, of the blue heron, paused for a long three seconds, and then barked him away.

No, I didn't believe it was Rajiv, just a wonderful coincidence. Aunt Eleanor believed. My mother believed. I wished I could believe.

Ma believed. When I told her about the second blue heron she said, "He has come back one last time to see his garden which he has loved so much." Matter-of-fact and calm as a marble Buddha. She told me that when her husband died, he came back to her as a crow who landed on her balcony and stayed until she fed him.

*

I oscillated between ground and air, an atheist dreaming of magic, both looking for and trying not to see the sleight-of-hand behind the trick.

When your laws of physics are suspended, when the unthinkable happens, when the deep injustice of death occurs, then you don't know what or how to believe anymore. Your world is refigured. All degrees of probability are leveled and anything could happen. Nothing and everything bears meaning. When the most overpoweringly present thing in your life is an absence, then meaning itself—the very meaning of meaning—takes wing. In this extraordinary realm after a death, where the most mundane object becomes significant—becomes, indeed a sign—and where the ephemera of life shimmer with portent, it's easy to believe in ghosts.

What is a ghost? Is it the victory of memory over reality, or memory's peripheral vision? Is it merely the residue of sensory perceptions that linger and linger, in defiance of neurons? Maybe a ghost is white paper dreaming in white, or the darkest night dreaming in black. Perhaps a ghost is a blue heron far from water.

Then I told myself no, we're not going to fly off into superstition and magic. Though I was raised Jewish and Raju Hindu, we'd struggled to find our own truths, uncomforting and uncomfortable though there were. Throughout the whole dying process, we were the supposedly mythical atheists in the foxhole, to the very end. I would dignify Rajiv's death by facing the truth head on, as he had.

But Rajiv's courage was far more capacious than mine, as was his imagination. His nonexistence was literally unimaginable to me. It was nearly impossible for me to think about his absence—so real, so *there*—without filling it with presence. It was impossible not to animate his loss with personal myths, not to look for movement in shadows, against the laws of gravity.

*

Ten days after Rajiv's death, under the piercing Colorado sun, I poured his ashes into a waterfall in Rocky Mountain National Park (surreptitiously, in case it violated any environmental regulations). The Hindu tradition that Rajiv had grown up in, and that my mother-in-law still breathed, required that the ashes go straight from the crematorium to a river. As my lapsed-Jewish atheism offered no objections to this practice, we decided on a setting that he'd loved. I knew it was exactly the right place even though he and I had never discussed the matter. When I'd asked Rajiv tentatively, months earlier, if he wanted his ashes to go back to the Ganges, as I'd assumed, he'd brushed the suggestion away with a flick of the wrist. "It's polluted enough already." He hadn't been that interested in the remains of his body, which bore no meaning to him, so I left all such decisions to his mother, who believed that the following of funerary rites affected the shape of Rajiv's next life.

Now, the waterfall spraying her starched white sari, Ma wailed as I patted the last of her son's remains out of the funeral home's box and into droplets.

I looked all over Rocky Mountain National Park for a blue heron, but couldn't find one anywhere. Not even lurking near water, where he should be.

*

I lurked on a chat room for young widows. One wrote, "It helps to talk with other dead people." Then in a new paragraph, "I see that was a slip. What I meant to say was, 'It helps to talk with other people living with death.'" But as is so often the case, the parapraxis is more accurate than the correction. We mourners are temporary zombies, half in the realm of death alongside our loved ones.

When I tell friends about my blue heron, a common reaction is, "You ask for a sign and you get the one you asked for. What more do you need?" They believe. But I don't.

Still—I regularly checked the fence from the bedroom window, hoping for him to come back.

*

In Zoroastrian tradition, the body is left on the roof of a Tower of Silence for vultures to pick clean. Now this practice has a different meaning for me, unmoored from its traditional cultural meaning. It incorporates the corpse into a thing of feathers, and brings the flesh, in pieces, into flight. It's not a mere metaphor for the soul flying up; the literal body itself, finally, flies.

At least the body can be useful, Rajiv would say. At least it can serve the cycle of life for a while longer.

But sometimes the physical world, with its laws of conservation of matter and energy, are not enough for us. We create a law of conservation of the soul, and believe that there is such a thing as a soul separable from a body and capable of outlasting its embodiment. We need to know that our soul, apart from the body, is recycled or preserved or "saved."

But it's the *body* that I miss, *his* body. The slightly duck-toed walk, dribbling an imaginary soccer ball. The taut thighs. The white appendectomy scar slowly fading into his cinnamon skin. The way his hands danced when he talked politics. The shoulders ready for a shrug. The sharp-edged smile that greeted particularly delicious ironies. What is a soul without a body? What is a soul, finally, if not embodiedness itself?

*

Thirteen days after death, in Hindu tradition, a Sraadh is held. My brother-in-law, Sujoy, orchestrated Rajiv's Sraadh in a grand temple in

New York and prepared a handout to explain the event to Rajiv's non-Hindu friends:

> It is believed in Hinduism that the departed soul travels through the *pretaloka* (the world of ghosts and spirits) to the *pitraloka* (the heaven or the world of ancestors), and several rituals are performed to aid this journey. As in most Hindu ceremonies, the process is initiated by elaborate offerings towards the various Gods and Goddesses.
>
> On the final day as per tradition, the spirits of predecessors in the family are invited to receive the soul of the deceased individual. They are symbolically offered food, clothes, water etc. and the completion of the ceremony is marked by the mergence of the deceased soul with those of its ancestors.

Mergence, he wrote, as if neither *emergence* nor *re-emergence* nor even *merging* quite met the moment. *Mergence*, more fact than act. A state of being that was both new and eternal.

During the ceremony, we all sat around a fire while a swami chanted in Hindi before a picture of Raju with a red dot on his forehead. Ma rocked back and forth, her face shrouded in white handkerchiefs as she sobbed. People came and went. Shadows shifted and shifted under the swaying sun. I felt like I was watching a foreign film without subtitles. Sujoy offered rounds of apples, bananas, mangoes, packets of underwear and undershirts, and starched white kurtas to beings outside of our known material world. It made as much and as little sense to me as anything else in the remaining material world.

At the conclusion of the ceremony for Rajiv's departed soul, the swami clicked and cooed. Out of nowhere came a swoop of large black birds. Ravens? Crows? The swami offered them food, which they sorted and stabbed at with their sharp black beaks. When they flew off Rajiv had symbolically joined his ancestors, with whom, it was hoped, he would rest in peace, not be swept back into the cycle of karma. Ma held out her arms to the retreating crows.

*

I lurked at my bedroom window, scanning the neighborhood for my blue heron. The more time went by, the more I needed his return. I stopped worrying about whether I believed or not. I strained for a sighting as the months crept towards the first *yahrzeit*.

*

When a sighting failed to materialize, I began to dig among reincarnation myths, telling myself that I was just visiting, and that my exploration was purely academic. A myth is a story a culture tells itself to create meaning where there is none. In this sense, all myths are creation myths, making light out of darkness and matter out of nothingness. Whether the story is true or false is irrelevant to its work as myth. Because the meaningless of death is humanly unacceptable, because nothingness is unthinkable, myths sprout from the burial grounds or funeral pyres of every culture. Perhaps religion itself exists, finally, to deal with the problem of death, to reckon with or perhaps to deny its reality and finality. At the very core of Christianity is the myth of redemption, positing that death is not death after all, that, in John Donne's words, "one short sleep past, we wake eternally, and Death shall be no more." In the ultimate oxymoron, it will be death itself that will die.

The most famous book of myths, Ovid's *Metamorphoses*, a first-century collection of stories of Roman gods and legends, teems with transformations among humans, gods, animals, plants, and inanimate Nature. Though suffused with love, lust, passion, and desire, the underlying theme of the collection is mortality. The cruelty of death and its partner, impermanence, only deepens amidst the amorous passions. The gods often turn humans—in order to keep them from dying or suffering—into objects of nature that eternally return. Sometimes the gods will transform a human into a plant or inorganic landscape: Daphne, to escape being raped by Apollo, is transformed into a laurel tree; Baucis and Philemon becoming intertwining trees before one of the married couple has to suffer the death of the other. But the figures of nature that humans (and gods) most commonly metamorphose into are winged: bats, eagles, owls, storks, swans, swallows, nightingales, crows, herons. Birds appear as omens and oracles, spirited messengers of the beyond.

In personal myths, too, there is a preponderance of flighted creatures— birds, butterflies, bugs, and angels. They live right alongside us but we generally fail to notice them—until we are looking for signs. Why do these creatures suggest themselves to us as metaphors? Is it because we can't accept that the physical world of gravity and increasing entropy is the end of it, or that our souls are a matter of worldly neurons alone? Does our instinct for transcendence recognize itself in the gravity-defying ascent created in an effortless flicker of light on wings? Perhaps it's no accident that the image of Christ that bears the most resonance—far more than any image of Jesus standing on the ground—is the one of him aboveground on the cross, arms outstretched, as if already in flight even as he died.

*

The most famous Ovidian myth may be that of Orpheus and Eurydice. When Eurydice dies on her wedding day, the gods allow her groom, Orpheus, to go down to Hades and return her to the world of the living—as long as he doesn't turn to look at his wife following behind him. But of course he can't stop himself. He has to look. That's how it is: you see them peripherally, and you know that you should enjoy the peripheral vision without getting greedy, that if you look directly at them you'll see it's not them after all. Hence the warning against looking behind. Best to feel their presence, not see the truth. Orpheus looks, and Eurydice disappears back into the underworld.

*

Three *yahrzeits* passed without any more blue heron sightings. I found my mind landing on an explanation. Both sightings had been within thirteen days; after that period, according to Hindu belief, Rajiv's soul would have moved on to its next life, and so he wouldn't be returning to send me signs anymore. Then I'd remind myself that I didn't believe in ghosts or reincarnation or trans-species metamorphoses, that the blue herons were not Rajiv. I knew that. Still, it would have been nice to have another sighting. In the absence of an organized religion to follow, I invented my own rituals or borrowed others. I lit *yahrzeit* candles on the eve of his death anniversaries, then spent the next day visiting his waterfall in Rocky Mountain National Park. On his birthdays I planted new perennials in his garden: lavenders, echinaceas, roses, and, once, an *"Anacyclus Depressus"*—a dry-climate perennial I discovered in the nursery and bought for the name (in recognition of the depression my grief had metamorphosed into), but it died before the summer was over. I waited for a sign. Mostly I missed him actively, missed him in the way that "to miss" can be a more active verb than "to dig" or "to plant." Sometimes "to wait" can be even more active than "to miss."

People told me it was time to "move on." I bristled at the term, with its embedded metaphor of linear movement towards a finish line. "Move," I might grant, but I rejected "move *on.*" I wasn't going anywhere. Why should grieving—why should life—be structured as a progress narrative? Maybe it should be more like the rhythm of a garden. A garden doesn't "move on." It reverts and renews.

I thought about getting a blue heron tattoo. I wanted to mark myself somehow, to mark my body, but lacked the institutionalized methods of religious tradition. I collected photos and paintings of blue herons, reminding myself that I didn't believe.

*

Three years after Rajiv's death and seventeen years after Uncle Bob's, I visited Aunt Eleanor in Miami Beach. As we walked down the street past the kosher bakery, Aunt Eleanor huddling in her turtleneck sweater under the blazing sun, a splat of white bird-dropping landed on her orange sleeve. Aunt Eleanor shook her fist at the bird on the telephone wire above us. "You stop that, Bob." She shook her fist one more time for good measure, and then turned to me. "Bob always did have a sense of humor."

*

Four years after Rajiv's death, my backyard neighbor, Tom, stood laughing on the other side of the tall fence that separates our very separate yards: mine, sere; his, the fruits of robust retirement years, luxuriant with exotic plants encircling a water pond. He was telling me about all the work that went into maintaining his pond, and all the mishaps that befell it. "One summer I even tried to keep koi fish." Though I hardly knew him, and he was perfectly affable, I didn't trust him; there was something hawk-like in his movements, and his dry laugh was more like a caw. But I had to ask, in spite of my instinct for self-preservation, "What happened?"

"Oh, they just attracted the herons, who made fast work of them." Tom laughed up phlegm, shrugged, and shook his head.

I didn't laugh; I liquefied. So there was a rational explanation, and my heron was merely predator, not harbinger. If I were a character in Ovid, I would transform into a waterfall. I saw the truth and lost my ghost.

*

Six years after Rajiv's death I visited my mother-in-law in Kolkata, where the caw of crows begins each morning and fills each day. It is the first sound of life after a monsoon. Even in a city where these black birds land on every available perch, an unusually large number seemed to crowd Ma's kitchen window with insistent squawking. When I asked her why, she said that they just seemed drawn to her. But then I caught her putting scraps out for them after a meal. The birds nearly attacked her hand along with the bowl the instant she placed it on the ledge. "Why shouldn't I feed my crows?" she said, embarrassed and defensive. "You have your blue heron."

Ma believes. She finds comfort in feeding the crows, her crows, who bear signs of her husband. She still believes that the blue heron is linked to Rajiv in some way. She tells me she must go to Rocky Mountain National Park to visit Rajiv one last time before she dies. A part of her still thinks her son is there, even while she also believes he's been reincarnated. She knows how to see by not looking, which has allowed her husband and her son to visit her every day since their deaths. I'm glad for Ma that she has her crows, for Cindy her ladybugs, and for Marge her nails and peacocks. But I no longer have my blue heron.

Has my husband visited me since he died? No. I tried to visit him, but not content to feel his presence, I turned to look, and he receded into the shadows. Now I have only memory—and an occasional ghostly sighting from memory's peripheral vision, which I no longer turn to look at directly, but let it sit at my side, just out of vision and reach. I am content, now, to linger in its lingering.

5/ See Monkey Dance, Make Good Photo

"Madam, Madam, see monkey dance." The monkey-wallah has caught sight of my white face outside the dining hall. He darts across the street in a lungi and flip-flops, his two monkeys scampering at his feet. I shake my head, but he persists. "See monkey dance, make veddy good photo." As he points to the camera in my hand, a crowd of dhotis and saris gathers around the monkeys and traps me in its circle.

The customs and immigrations forms that the airline attendants had distributed on the Air India flight had asked me to identify the reason for my visit, but none of the options seemed appropriate to check off (or "tick," as Rajiv would have called it). Not Business, not Transit, Official, Employment, Education, Conference, Medical Treatment, or Sport. That left Tourism, Social, and Pilgrimage. I didn't want to be a tourist, with that term's orientalist connotations, suggesting someone who travels to South Asia, on pilgrimages or spiritual journeys, in quest of enlightenment or exoticism, and, visiting temples or ashrams and the occasional slum, reduces the whole country of India to a single word like "Pray." The tourist's India is the Taj Mahal and the kama sutra; it's elephants and peacocks and dancing monkeys. Way back when I'd first started dating Rajiv, when we hung out in Valhalla, the underground graduate student bar—me, a suburban white girl studying literature; Rajiv a foreign student in environmental engineering—a fellow grad student, an American, had said to Rajiv, "Your culture is so spiritual." Rajiv had laughed so hard that beer trickled out his nose. Now I know why. After thirteen years with Rajiv, I couldn't be just a tourist.

So, Social or Pilgrimage? I checked Social, which missed the mark, because I also couldn't allow myself to think of this trip as a pilgrimage. No, I wasn't in search of Rajiv. I knew very well that he wouldn't be waiting for me in India, if I only looked in the right places.

Ostensibly I was in India to visit my in-laws. I'd been to Kolkata (back when it was still called Calcutta) twice before—thirteen and then ten years earlier—with my Bengali husband, who was born and raised here. I'd met him in graduate school, and then, after being academic gypsies for several years, we'd settled into Colorado as assistant professors. But then Rajiv got sick. Then very sick. Suddenly, he had Stage IV (terminal) colon cancer, and within eleven months he was dead, three days after turning thirty-eight. I went on another journey altogether then, to a place both underground and unearthly. Now, six years later, I was emerging, which friends mistook for "moving on." My brother-in-law and his wife, who now lived in the U.S., were visiting my mother-in-law for the summer and had asked me to join them for the reunion.

Six years is unacceptably long for an American to grieve. My culture denies death more anxiously than repressed memories, and deems mortality far more taboo and pornographic than sex. Because my American friends, even my grief counselor, found my extended grieving abnormal and morbid, I'd been hiding it. But India, I knew, would be different. This culture appreciated death's ubiquity. Hinduism, the majority religion, even incorporates death into its cast of divine characters. Bengalis especially worship Kali, great mother in the house of death.

India would be hard for me. I recognized that. I'd hear all new stories and memories of Rajiv from his relatives and friends, and I'd realize anew the weight of my loss. We'd only lived in Colorado three years before Rajiv got sick, so it had quickly forgotten him. But his corner of India would want to reclaim him.

Then too, I would see Rajiv everywhere. Even back home in Northern Colorado, there was an Indian man I'd regularly run into on campus in the years after Rajiv's death. Not only did he have Rajiv's build—slim but sturdy from years of childhood soccer—but he had Rajiv's walk: tight, rigid shoulders reconciling with relaxed hips, and steps that were both dragging and precise. It was a third-world walk, one I'd seen commonly in Kolkata, but rarely in the States, a walk that came from tramping in the swelter through dirt roads in flat leather sandals, keeping movements minimal with a grace disguised as laziness. When I saw this man from behind, my abdomen tightened, and I had to see him from the front, to verify that it wasn't Rajiv. I *knew* it wasn't Rajiv, *of course* it wasn't Rajiv—I'd witnessed both his death and his cremation, the two most absolutely real moments of my life—but still I had to rush ahead and turn for a glimpse of this man's face. But when he cocked his head for an explanation, I couldn't say, "Just making sure that you're not my dead husband." So I said nothing. I wonder if he could see on my face, along with the embarrassment and, perhaps, a touch of relief, that fresh hit of grief. As if a bit of stow-away hope had found harbor in my heart despite my best policing efforts.

That's what I expected to be most difficult about India—seeing Rajiv everywhere, and experiencing his death in repeated aftershocks. But what turned out to be difficult was the opposite. Rajiv was not everywhere. He wasn't anywhere.

The monkey-wallah squats, and begins to chant in Bengali. The two monkeys step forward, revealing their heavy metal collars and cantilevered chains. The man taps on a drum, and the monkeys dutifully stand and bounce, their bodies festive, their faces impassive.

Then I realize that there are actually three monkeys; the smaller monkey is supporting an even smaller one, a baby, which clings to her belly and fingers a nipple.

After Rajiv died, I couldn't bring myself to go alone to gatherings put on by the local Indian association. I especially missed the Durga Puja, so important to Bengalis, with its gigantic idols in intense, psychedelic colors of purples and golds and more shades of hot pink or magenta or fuchsia than I knew names for. Without knowing why, I'd always been drawn to Durga, an aspect of the fierce goddess Kali and a definitive goddess for Bengalis, Rajiv included. He had collected a few Durga/Kali brass figurines, and after his death I grouped them into a little shrine in awed recognition of the power of this warrior goddess. Adding more icons to the shrine and disguising it as kitsch, I hid my worship of Kali from my academic friends; among the worst offenses of orientalism is appropriating bits and pieces of another culture's mythologies for one's own uses without regard to their proper contexts. But my Kali shrine put a shape to the incomprehensible injustice of death, to the senseless and arbitrary forces of destruction. Of course I pulled her out of her own cultural context and shoved her into mine, projecting my own personal myths onto her along the way. As an outsider, bereft of my Indian community, I'd never again get my chance to learn what she meant to true Hindus, outside of books. That, too, was part of my loss. So, although I knew I was appropriating Kali in that icky way that white Western women feel empowered to do, I needed her. She felt more true to me than any of the gods of my own culture.

And I missed my culture-in-law, which had become my outlawed home. When I saw gatherings of Indians on campus or in restaurants, and heard the singing rhythms of their many languages—Hindi, Bengali, Telagu, Malayalm, Marathi, Punjabi, all of which sounded the same to me when spoken at native speeds—I ached a little, longing to belong. When the organizers of the India Association of Northern Colorado met at a local coffee shop on Friday nights, planning their events in an English-accessorized Hindi, jokingly calling each other "boss" and "guru," I lingered at a neighboring table, floating in their lilting waves of language.

For six years, every whiff of incense, or clink of bangles on a woman's wrist, or taste of turmeric or cumin, would whet the ache.

Arriving at my mother-in-law's house in Kolkata, that longing intensified. Before jet lag cleared enough to separate day from night, relatives began appearing at Ma's door. Boromama, the patriarch, and his wife Boromami, now both in their seventies. Chotomama, whose bigamy was an open secret. Chotomami, whose vitiligo had progressed significantly over the last ten years, making her white patches paler than my pink skin. Cousins, twice- and thrice-removed, who counted as immediate family to Bengalis and called me "cousin-sister." Even Rajiv's father's brother's son's wife came to see me. As each entered, I readied myself for the battle against tears—theirs, mine. But that's not the way it went. Instead, they talked to my in-laws in Bengali the whole time, occasionally glancing at me or nodding in my direction. Rajiv had told me that many of his less educated relatives were embarrassed by their English, and that my being an English professor didn't help. But I think, too, that they saw my inability to speak Bengali as a character flaw in me, which it was my responsibility, not theirs, to overcome.

I'd tried to learn Bengali when Rajiv was alive. He taught me words like *klantho* (tired) and *mishti* (sweet), and a few phrases like *ki kircheesh?* (whatya doing?) and *ami tomai koop bhalobashi* (I love you very much) and *amar mishti pode* (my sweet ass). But mostly Rajiv got impatient when I tried to practice *Bangla* and switched to English. My Bengali acquisition stagnated at the level of basic dog training, as I mostly just practiced on my three dogs, whom I called, alternately, *bhalo kukur!* (good dog) and *bajay kukur!* (bad dog). A common cry at the dinner table was "*bas!*" (enough) when, true to their spaniel natures, they hounded us for food. After Rajiv died, after the dogs mourned in dog-time and then bounded back to life just as my own mourning became real, I continued to speak Bengali to them. I even tried to get tutored by a native speaker, but when she taught me the alphabet, the 50 odd characters all looked the same, and my hand fumbled like a kindergartner's trying to form letters I couldn't recognize. So when conversations now switched to Bengali, and then when my in-laws, along with their visitors to Jodhpur Park, abandoned English altogether, I understood how my dogs at home must feel all the time: trying to read body language, looking for a decodable sign amidst the general meaninglessness.

When I lay in bed at night back home in Colorado, I used to take comfort in remembering Rajiv's body, spooning me from behind; with my eyes closed I could make him present at my back. But I'd started losing the substance of the memory, the exact weight of his arm slotted over my waist, the geography of callouses inside his hand, the way he moved it slowly to press against my thigh, the precise texture of his parting lips when I rolled over into him, the distinct taste of his tongue. All I had left was a ghost kiss.

In bed at night in India, amid the last caws of crows, the dying horn honks, the moon-howls of street dogs—the perfect backdrop for the return of memory—Rajiv did not come back to me. Mosquitoes came, and spiders, and, once, a lizard. That was all.

But the coming reunion lunch would feed the memories, if I could just hold out. My brother- and sister-in-law were organizing it, and I was helping to pay for it. They'd rented a commercial dining hall and caterers, and had invited all members of the extended family residing in West Bengal. They'd even had hot pink napkins printed up in lacy white lettering, conveying the message "With Family Happy Times. Enjoy! Sujoy, Joya, and Debby." With family, I would remember.

The larger monkey turns to face me. Hanging loosely from his shoulders is what was once a toddler's sports jersey, now grimy and tattered. The stencil against the orange fabric is peeling, but I can still make out the black and white tessera of a soccer ball. Even through his impassive face the monkey looks miserable. The man calls out a command to him, and he pulls back his lips. The man calls again, and the monkey bats his eyes, almost coquettishly. The crowd laughs. Beating a drum and chanting louder, the man gives the chain a yank, and the monkey does a back flip. "Ah," the crowd sighs, and the man makes the monkey do it twice more until it produces applause.

The female monkey is free of the humiliation of human toddler clothing, probably to enable her to suckle her infant. The monkeys don't resist their roles—they pull on their metal collars and clasps with dexterous fingers, like businessmen adjusting their ties, trying to pry them unobtrusively a few millimeters looser. The baby is not collared, and from time to time wan-

ders from the mother, but always returns to her arms. When the man sees
me looking at the female he yanks on her chain, starts singing, and yanks
again. The female shakes. It's supposed to simulate dancing, I assume, but
it is a hideous shaking, as she holds tight to the baby on her belly to keep its
head from snapping while its teeth chatter to the monkey-wallah's chants.

On the day of the reunion lunch I put on the pink salwar-kameez
that I'd first worn ten years earlier. My mother-in-law had bought the
outfit for me to wear at a luncheon she hosted on my first visit to India
to celebrate Rajiv's and my recent wedding. I'd brought my white salwar-
kameez set, intricately bejeweled, but Ma shuddered in horror when I
told her I planned to wear it. "White is the color of death," Rajiv had
explained. "Bad luck to wear it at a marriage celebration."

The pink kameez I wore instead was hand-embroidered with white
thread in an intricate paisley pattern. If you looked closely, the teardrop
shapes turned into birds looking backward past their tail feathers. I don't
usually wear pink, but that first time I wore the outfit I felt beautiful.
Relatives complimented Rajiv on his fair-skinned wife, and deliberately
mispronounced Debby as "Devi" (goddess), which disturbed Rajiv and
me just a little, back when we had the luxury of being disturbed by things
like colonialist beauty aesthetics.

But at today's "Happy Times" luncheon, I was not a goddess, not a
new family member, but a widow, an outsider. I realized too late that
I was probably expected to wear white this time. After a few pleasant
greetings to me in English—How are you keeping? How is your mother?
What time do you go in to work in the morning? What do you pack for
lunch?—they turned to Bengali, and I sat alone, playing my game of trying to pick out words. At one point I was relieved by Boromami, who,
never one to feel shame at her English or anything else, chatted with me
briefly. "You are looking so sickly-sickly, so pulled down. You must put
on ten pounds to lose some of your wrinkles. Fatten your face. A balloon
does not wrinkle." Boromami was going deaf, so she didn't pause for a
reply. "You must eat more. Have another rasagola."

Not a single relative—most of whom I'd last seen with Rajiv here ten years ago—talked about Rajiv, or even about his loss. There was not even a mention of Rajiv's name among friends or relatives. I would have been able to pick it out amidst the Bengali. When I mentioned him—"Rajiv used to speak very highly of you" or "Rajiv cared about you very deeply"— anything to bring his name into the room—they looked away or changed the subject, often with more questions: What time are you leaving for work in the morning? How far is your work? What do you cook for dinner? Why must you keep so many dogs? I sought some evidence of Rajiv in their faces, some sign that he was remembered, that his loss was present amidst the bright silks and brown curries and magenta napkins. But Kolkata, too, had forgotten. The only person who wanted to talk about him was Ma, but when she did, her living son scolded her for being morbid, for holding on to the past and to pain, for failing to "move on."

How dare my brother-in-law—or any of us—move on? How dare Kolkata keep progressing? Six years ago, at Rajiv's *sraadh*, some of these relatives told me through tears that they would never forget Rajiv, and I knew they meant it when they said it. But now, not only had they forgotten about Rajiv, they'd even forgotten about his absence. As if Rajiv had never existed. I was being unfair to Rajiv's relatives, I knew, but I didn't care. There was something entirely amoral, something cruel and awesome, in the way life goes on.

Ganesha, Shiva, Hanuman the monkey-god, and the ten-armed Kali danced in bronze at the four corners of the dining hall. As I struggled to swallow the oily curries that left my lips slimy but dry, I looked especially at Kali, my goddess of destruction and rage and death, who wanders the cremation grounds with her bloodthirsty tongue. I admired her necklace of skulls—fifty skulls, legend has it, for the fifty letters of the Sanskrit alphabet—and her skirt of dismembered arms, fringed with fingers.

After I ate all I could manage, I went outside. I'd study the street dogs, I thought, to try to calm myself. Animals always help. I was fed up with my relatives who were no longer my relatives, fed up with my culture-in-law that was no longer my culture-in-law, fed up with the curries, the clothes, the all-too-humanness, the gods. All except Kali. I was keeping Kali.

Around the corner from the dining hall, a homeless man stood eating, from the top of the dumpster, the first round of waste from our reunion dinner. Two street dogs, mangy third-world mutts, waited beside him. The man looked almost like a sadhu, nearly naked, with only a loincloth-like dhoti and his long, matted hair to protect his skin. He chanted to himself between nervous jerks as he ferreted through the dumpster above the dogs' reach. Intermittently, he handed them a bit of the food he picked out of the remains. The female grabbed it from the male, trotted down the street with it, and threw her head back, chewing, before both dogs returned to the garbage bin and foraged alongside the man. The three worked silently together.

Shocks of hot pink studded the dumpster. The dogs licked at the pink napkins (my dogs at home would have swallowed them whole), and the man felt them for bits of fish bones, gristle, and rinds buried in their folds. Grease spots or worse covered every iteration of "With Family Happy Times." I pulled out my camera, whose memory card had plenty of space for the photos of relatives I wasn't going to be taking, and took pictures of these three stray creatures calmly picking at our ridiculously, offensively festive napkins. I, too, felt ridiculous, offensive even, in the lavishly embroidered pink salwar-kameez of my marriage celebration, so ironically inappropriate for this anti-marriage, this losing of my culture-in-law.

Inside the dining hall, I could see through the window, my relatives had all gone back for seconds of my brother-in-law's fish, mutton curry, curds, sweets, and Chotomami's hand-rolled pan. They adjusted their petticoat or pajama strings to make room for expanding waists.

That's when I heard *Madam, Madam*, when I was commanded in probably the only English the monkey-wallah knew to *See monkey dance, make veddy good photo.*

Shaking my head does no good. I want to tell the man to stop torturing his monkeys, that I'll pay him to keep them from dancing. But my gestures only produce more tricks, and my turning away raises the monkey-wallah's desperation. He orders the male to balance on a cane-length stick. I don't know what to do. "Photo, Madam," he orders me. So I take the photo, occupying my role as dutifully as the monkeys take up theirs, glad at least that the camera covers my eyes. I will go back home to the States as just another white woman with a good photo of a dancing monkey.

I realize that the only way to make the show stop is to pay the monkey-wallah, to be complicit in this miserable business. I fumble with my wallet to retrieve a colorful bill. The monkey-wallah commands the male monkey to snatch the hundred-rupee bill from my hand, and then throw it to the ground angrily, as if insulted by such a meager offering. The crowd laughs. I take out another bill and hand it to the monkey. The monkey-wallah, satisfied, pockets the bills the monkey hands him, and turns his chanting to other onlookers.

Here in this moment I vow to myself never to come back to India, except maybe for Ma's funeral. Or if I do, I tell myself, I get to be the tourist, the ugly American, alternately gawking and exoticizing.

But of course I already am that person. Why did I think India would be more spiritual? Why did I think my Bengali relatives would be more accepting of the presence of death? Just because they worship Kali-ma standing iconically with her necklace of skulls over her supine lover, Shiva?

Maybe I needed to come all the way to India to find out that India wasn't holding out on me, that it wasn't a pilgrimage, that Rajiv wasn't here waiting to be recovered. Maybe it was like my need to look at Rajiv's doppelganger on campus; I needed to look at India, this strangely familiar stranger, to know it wasn't mine.

While the monkey-wallah is turned away, the male wanders to me and presses his hands to my pink kameez. With delicate fingers, he picks at a bit of the white embroidery, inquisitively, almost longingly. There's something tender in the way he plucks the needlework at the edge of my kameez, in the way he traces the pattern with his finger and then tries to close his hand around it as if catching the embroidered bird in his palm. For the briefest moment, I can feel the soft pressure of his hand on my thigh.

Then the monkey-wallah sees, and yanks the monkey back. The monkey's hand shoots to his neck at the sting of this force beyond his understanding, arbitrary and senseless. His pink fingers curl around the metal.

6/ For the Polar Bears

"That methane gas from cows is the worst," Rhonda says from the butt-buster. She shoots her leg backwards like a mule kicking a bucket behind her, again and again.

At Curves, a gym for gym-resistant middle-aged women, we talk our way through a half-hour of interval training. The exercise machines are arranged in a circle facing inward, and every thirty seconds we rotate. During our two laps around the circuit, we talk about everything from our children or pets to our wayward bodies to tomorrow's weather to climate change.

Rhonda's been worrying about carbon emissions.

"Methane from cows?" Judy asks from her trainer's spot in the center of the circuit. All machines face her.

"From the farts," I add helpfully from the stairstepper.

"Change stations now," the woman's recorded voice instructs through the speakers. We change.

"Cow flatulence causes global warming?" Judy asks.

Judy and I have both "lost" our husbands. That's how the women here at Curves put it; no-one uses the word "widow." Saying we "lost" our husbands suggests that we're wandering around looking for them, and yet we were both right there when they died, and right there again when the remains of our respective husbands were put to rest, Tim underground, Rajiv in an incinerator. We know right where our husbands are. It's our own bodies we've lost—and maybe our selves, too, a bit.

Judy took up her job as a Curves trainer just over a year after her forty-five-year-old husband stroked out on a treadmill stress test. In that year, she's added a blanket of flesh over her core of hard muscle. I went in the other direction, letting my body eat itself up. It's as if our bodies grieve by mimicking our husbands' last days. I'm a year younger than Judy, but six years ahead of her in the grieving game, and hoping to put some meat back on my bones.

A surprisingly high proportion of women at Curves are widows. Maybe widows, not ready for the meat market, are more likely to work out at a women-only gym. Or maybe men just die off quicker.

Rhonda, post-mastectomy and post-chemo, is on the other side of cancer, which led to her new-found environmentalism. Her prosthetic breast wanders around her chest during her work-out as she tells us about factory farms and Americans' unsustainable diets, about the petroleum that goes into the fertilizer to produce the corn to feed the cows. About feedlot bloat from this unnatural diet. About how the cows are packed into stalls so tight they can't turn around, and stand knee-deep in their own manure. How behind each bit of beef we eat is an ungodly amount of suffering, and of oil, and of gas. "We're eating our way to flooded coastlines and lost islands and extinct species. Look at the polar bears."

"What about the polar bears?" Judy asks. "I like polar bears."

"The arctic icecaps are melting. Their habitat."

Judy looks to me for confirmation. My knowledge of global warming is shaky, despite Rajiv's career as an environmental engineer. I wish I could ask him. Instead, I just nod.

"So my nightly McDonald's drive-through is killing polar bears?"

"Nightly?" Rhonda frowns.

"What I do is, I buy two Big Macs, then I take the buns off one and put the insides into the other. I eat in the car, so I don't have to face the empty chair at the kitchen table. I know, I know, I'm eating my way back to Tim. If I stuff down enough burgers, maybe I can join him soon."

She pauses while the voice tells us to change stations. We change. I'm now on the adductor, mimicking a gynecological exam to work my inner thighs.

"That's a lot of beef," Rhonda says.

"I know. When they do my autopsy they're going to find golden arches squeezing my heart in a hammer-hold. But I love my beef. It's all I got left."

Talk of beef makes me salivate, but in a pre-nausea way. I haven't eaten beef since Rajiv died seven years ago. Maybe I gave it up out of respect for his Hinduism and environmentalism. Maybe there was something else, too. Something about the way the smell of singed fat made me think of incineration. Something about the way a slab of beef resembled a corpse. I swallow.

"New Year's is coming up," Rhonda says. "Time for resolutions."

"But *beef*," Judy says. "My comfort food."

"Have you ever seen a baby polar bear?" Rhonda asks.

"Yes," Judy sighs. "All flapping paws tripping over themselves." Judy can tear up instantaneously. She can laugh and cry at the same time. It sounds like a gurgle.

"Change stations now," the voice demands. We change.

*

"I've gone seven days without beef," Judy says from the center of the circle in early January.

"Good for you," I say from the obliques. I'm working on my love handles.

"It's for the polar bears," Judy says. "If it were for myself, I'd keep eating my way to Tim."

"What do polar bears have to do with beef?" Bev asks from the pec dec. Bev, a septuagenarian, chews gum throughout her work-out. It's the only way she can last for half an hour without a cigarette.

"Cow farts are melting the ice caps," Judy explains. "The Papa bears go out to forage, and then their ice floes break off and they can't return to their families. Everybody starves." She looks to me again for support.

"More or less," I mumble, making my love handles bulge and tauten, bulge and tauten. When Rajiv and I walked side-by-side, arms around each other's waists, we would squeeze the other's fleshy excess. Then cancer etched out his ribs and ate away his stomach, till all that was left to hold onto was hipbone.

Bev looks unconvinced. "That doesn't sound right." She chews thoughtfully.

"It's not right," Judy says. "It's just not right at all." That liquid laugh again. "You know what else isn't right? If I can give up my burgers for the polar bears, why couldn't Tim give up his junk food for me?"

"May I ask what was the cause of your husband's death?" Bev asks.

"Pepperoni pizzas," Judy laughs again, wetly, grimly. "French fries. Cheese fucking Danish." She turns to me. "I guess this is the anger stage, huh?"

"Change stations now," the voice says. We change.

"I'll tell you, though," Judy turns back to me. "Now that I've gone semi-vegetarian, I have some real flatulence issues myself. Did that happen to you? Your whole gut rebels? Wouldn't that be counter-productive?"

"I don't think it's just the farts producing all the greenhouse gases," I say.

"No," Judy agrees. "It's also the belches."

*

One thing you miss when your life partner dies is having someone to buy presents for. Even just the small gag gift that betokens the shared inside joke. So when I saw the polar bear bath toy, modeled after a rubber duckie, I had to get it for Judy. It gives a desperately gleeful squeak as, handing it to her, I press the rounded tummy. It was designed to float on its back, belly up.

Judy's eyes do their quick-fill when I present it. You miss getting presents, too.

The polar bear's polyurethane eyes bulge, dead black, under her squeeze. "It's been thirteen days," Judy says. "Thirteen long beefless days. For you, little guy." She tickles the polar bear's belly with an index finger.

Rhonda's here today. "You might just as well put the polar bear in the toilet rather than the bathtub," she says, rising from the shoulder press and returning her errant breast. "The polar bears are doomed to die out, no matter what you do. It's only a matter of time. Do we give them seventy-five years, or only fifty years, before we melt all the ice caps."

"But I've stopped eating beef!" Judy is trying to joke. This is Curves; keep it light.

"Even if everyone in the world stopped eating beef, even if we all went vegan and Amish, it's still too late. You might as well just eat polar bear burgers directly."

"That can't be right," Judy tries again. "There must be something we can do to save the polar bears. I'm going to research it."

Rhonda shrugs. Judy squeezes the polar bear duckie so gently that its former squeak becomes a long, cartoonish moan.

"I do miss my beef," Judy says to the toy. "I miss my McDs. Every minute of every day." Her laugh is as moist as her eyes. She pats her own belly, which, despite its burger deprivation, keeps growing, threatening to overtake her whole body.

"Change stations now," says the voice from above.

*

"It's true," Judy says next time I enter the gym. "Papa bear is not coming home."

"Huh?"

"Rhonda's right. The polar bears are doomed. I did a search. They've got maybe 50 years. Can you imagine? A whole majestic species gone, just like that, just so we can eat burgers. Did you know that newborn polar bears come out smaller than human infants? Then they grow to three or four times heavier even than me. But when they're first born they're like cocker spaniel puppies." I think she's about to cry, without her usual accompanying laugh. A brief inconsolable sadness passes over her face. All I can do is hug her. Her flesh is layers and layers of soft, so different from the body of Rajiv that I hugged at the end, the body that my own still holds in muscle memory. "I know the nature of life is change," she says. "But there's got to be something more that we can do."

I ask Judy if she's still going to eat beef, now that it's hopeless. But she shakes her head. "I know the polar bears are doomed. I accept that. But maybe we can give them a few more days."

I remember Rajiv's final days. We would have done anything, paid anything, for a few more.

"How long have you been beefless?" I ask.

"Thirty days. And thirty nights. But you've been beefless much longer."

"Years."

"It gets easier?"

"A little."

I resume my place on the circuit. Climbing into the ab/back machine, I suck in my stomach like I'm about to be punched, and I bow into the abdominal crunch, my body embracing the slow burn of disappearance, until the woman's voice commands us, once again, to change stations now.

7/ The Other Thompson

I distinctly remember hearing of the event the way some people remember learning of the JFK assassination or of 9/11. It was October 18, 2011. I'd turned on the car radio and had just begun to back out of my driveway when the announcer reported the shootings—the bears, the wolves, and the lions. A man in Zanesville, Ohio named Terry Thompson, who had a personal zoo of fifty-two exotic animals, unbolted or cut open all of their cages and then shot himself. Police, realizing the impossibility of rescuing the animals before dusk, began shooting them. As I sat horrified in my driveway, my dogs watching me from the living room window, tallies rolled in: eighteen tigers killed, seventeen lions, six black bears, two grizzlies, two wolves...

By the next morning, nearly all of Thompson's animals were dead, at least forty-eight of them shot by police. Some animal rights advocates condemned these shootings, likening the officers to big game hunters, referring to the scene as an "urban safari". Defenders of the police countered that once the animals were released the humans had little choice, and that Thompson must have known he was dooming to death the animals he claimed to love. I remember seeing police officers talking on television; even the ones certain they did the right thing shielded horror behind their eyes. And I remember the images of the animals. One photo in particular, which soon flew around the world, showed rows of lion and tiger carcasses covering the killing fields.

Even though I'm a teacher, the event hit me harder than the many
mass school shootings that have occurred before and since. It felt oddly
personal. Maybe that was simply because I share a last name with Terry
Thompson, and could be distantly related. Also I grew up in Ohio and
had passed through Zanesville. My connection to the story felt deeper,
though. I immersed myself in news of the incident, snapping up every
item I could find, but when I tried to talk to friends about it, few felt
connected to or even knew of the event. It was sad, they'd say, but at least
no humans died (not counting Thompson). The victims were, after all,
"only" animals. Why wasn't I more personally upset by the massacre of
humans in the Congo or our bombing of *human* civilians in Afghani-
stan? Why didn't I care more about my own species?

Over the days and weeks following the Zanesville catastrophe, people began to characterize Thompson as evil. One radio talk show host
labeled Thompson "asshole of the year." Callers said he must have hated
his animals, first to keep them in cages, and then to "free" them to certain death. I shared their outrage. But I was also feeling something else.
Thompson's condition felt too familiar for comfort.

My sympathy for the other players in the event had come easily. I
found myself imagining the 911 dispatcher's mounting realization as she
answered call after call reporting lion and tiger sightings. I could connect
with the burden that animal celebrity Jack Hanna must have felt as he
advised the police authorities, and with horrified cops forced to shoot
those massive, majestic animals. But I could also feel for Thompson, this
man to whom I felt uncannily related.

At the same time, I couldn't get that damn photo of the massacre out
of my head.

So when I learned that there was an exotic animal sanctuary not forty-
five minutes southeast of me that rescued animals like Terry Thompson's,
I had to go. I needed a happier image to displace the photo of killing
fields of lion and tiger carcasses that still haunted me.

Or so I told myself, but something else was going on too. The more I
read about tigers, the more I wanted to get up close to them.

"I'm not going to get eaten, am I?" My friend Kelley pretends he's joking, but he folds his arms tightly over his chest. We're entering The Wild Animal Sanctuary, a refuge for exotic animals in Keenesburg, Colorado, where we will tread along ramps above sharp-toothed, half-ton carnivores. In the parking lot, Kelley and I can already smell a funky, musky odor that can't be attributed to mere manure. We've brought enough gear—cameras, binoculars, water bottles, power bars, sunscreen, insect repellent—for a week-long safari. We're used to spending our weekends prowling thrift shops and antique malls, not scouting tigers. But on this perfect Saturday morning in May we're walking the plank.

The Wild Animal Sanctuary, or TWAS, features a "Mile Into the Wild" walkway, a ramp raised eighteen to forty-two feet in height, which stretches across 4,800 feet of the 720-acre sanctuary housing over 290 large carnivores. A guide briefs us at the entrance, telling us not to run or make loud noises. The animals have no natural predators who attack them from above, but they can still get threatened by overhead rumblings.

Then she gets to "the most important part." All of these animals were "born in captivity" and wouldn't survive in the wild, so taking refuge at the sanctuary was their best option. "We do NOT advocate keeping these animals as pets." She explains the history of some of these animals. Some came from ignorant individuals who tried to raise wild animals in garages or basements. Most of the lions, tigers, bears, wolves, and other exotic animals were rescued from horrendous living conditions. Often, they were kept as pets in cages. Sometimes they were raised for the underground pelt trade. They arrived at the sanctuary malnourished, sometimes declawed or even defanged, unsocialized, and miserable.

"How could anyone do that to an animal?" Kelley whispers to me. Around us other visitors shake their heads in disgust and disbelief.

These animals, the guide explains, could never be returned to the wild. They wouldn't survive. Even the ones who weren't defanged and declawed had never developed the proper hunting and social skills. So these animals, all neutered on arrival except for the male lions (who need their testosterone to maintain their glorious manes), would live out the rest of their lives in this sanctuary, where they could at least run around and mix with other members of their species. Bottom line, loud and clear: wild animals should never be kept as pets.

Then the guide sets us loose.

Just past the preview gathering we hit a sign announcing Servals.

"What's a serval?" Kelley asks.

"It's a kind of wild cat, isn't it?" I guess.

Kelley whips out his iPhone and googles. Servals come from Africa, where their 25- to 40-pound bodies hunt the savannas for rodents. They're aided by hypersensitive ears, so large in relation to their faces that they look like permanent kittens. The backs of their ears display little ocelli, or mock eyes, to fake out predators behind them. We train our binoculars on these sleeping, nocturnal creatures. Slowly we make out a cat, then two, then three. They suggest large, leggy housecats, or mini-leopards.

"They look like they could do some damage," Kelley says.

The servals had been kept as "pets," we read from the placard. One, kept in a New York apartment, grew unruly, so the owner filed down the feline's teeth and de-clawed her. When the cat still proved unmanageable, the owner surrendered her. The other cats had similar stories, but without the medieval torture techniques. That's horrible, we concur. These animals clearly need space to run and hunt. Again, the take-away was clear: servals should not, and cannot, be made into pets.

Farther down the ramp, a roving volunteer, another bubbly twenty-something woman, asks a little boy if he has any questions. "Do you have cheetahs?" the boy asks.

The guide says no.

"Is that because they're too quick to capture?"

"No, it's…"

The father steps in. "Where would someone get one of these animals? Like where are these people getting these animals?"

The guide laughs nervously. "Different places."

The father persists. "But, like, where would I go to get, say, a pet cheetah?"

"I wouldn't recommend it." The guide is on alert.

"No, no, no. Of course not," the father reassures her.

"Oh, okay," says the guide. "You sounded a little too interested for a minute there."

"No, I'm just wondering. Just say I were going to get a cheetah? Where would I go?"

The guide clamps down her jaw. "Black market," she says through her teeth.

As I researched Terry Thompson and animal hoarding, I learned that exotics ownership in the U.S. is far more common than you might think. There are more tigers in captivity in just the U.S. today than exist in the wild world-wide. Across this country, backyards and garages and basements hold exotics of all kinds: lions and tigers and bears, of course, but also giraffes, zebras, chimpanzees, hyenas, gazelles, lynx, kangaroos, and a surprising number of orangutans, lemurs, alligators, cobras, pythons, pangolins, and Komodo dragons. Just for starters. The breeding and trade of exotics is big business, and while it's largely gone underground now due to increasing regulations, it's still thriving.

The animals, of course, rarely thrive.

Nor is the impulse to own wildness particular to contemporary Americans; references to the captivation of animals stretch back through history. Exotic animal hoarding had long been understood as a sign of evil or, relatedly, a display of power: consider the fabled pet lion accompanying Ramses II into battle; or the biblical lions of Darius's "den," gazing at Daniel; or Nero's beloved tigress Phoebe, his alter-id, said to feed on his human enemies; or the rhinoceroses, elephants, lions, and bears roaming the Coliseum in the Roman Empire's staged hunts (which we would now call "trophy hunting"). Contemporary cases also abound. In Lawrence Anthony's *Babylon's Ark* I read about the rescue of Uday Hussein's private zoo of exotic carnivores, rumored to have fed on the human flesh of Hussein's enemies but left to starve when Hussein evacuated Baghdad. Most recently, drug dealers are reputed to have moved beyond pit bull terriers as status symbols to lions, tigers, and panthers. (There was even a *Law and Order* episode featuring this scenario.)

In fact, there seems to be an uncanny overlap between exotic animal collecting and imperialism, cultural critics have noted. Colonizers regularly brought back live trophies (humans as well as non-human animals) from the lands they dominated, in part as proof of mastery, but also as objects of curiosity. It's no mere coincidence, some scholars argue, that the era of global imperialism overlaps with the heyday of empiricism, with its appetite for knowing the unknown. Both share a limitless acquisitiveness. The notoriously bizarre Victorian menageries, containing such "curiosities" as big cats, baboons, orangutans, peacocks, even anteaters, provide mascots for an era of European consumption of Africa, Asia, and Australia. Critics of modern zoos and circuses, similarly, see these places as embodiments of humans' will to power/knowledge. We've told ourselves our desire to understand other species justifies forcing animals into captivity. Our contemporary culture translates desire into consumerism, telling us that if we love something, we should own it. We express our desire for the wild by consuming it.

Still, I sense something else, too, lying beyond this well-criticized acquisitiveness, cruelty, and the will to power/knowledge commonly understood as key motivations. Something even more destructive but more difficult simply to condemn.

As Kelley and I keep walking the Wild Animal Sanctuary's bridge, suddenly, *Holy Shit*, there's a tiger right below us. Then, all at once, many tigers. I can tell they're huge, even at this distant height above them. When they're not pacing, they can stand still as statues, which makes them all the more threatening. Their paws flex big as dinner plates, and their bellies slosh from side to side.

"Oh!" Kelley squeaks.

"Magnificent," I whisper.

We're the tiger's first visitors of the day. Several tigers stand, not facing us, but at maybe a forty-five degree angle, pulling their lips back so far from their teeth they show gums.

"They're smelling you," says a guide. "They smell through their mouths."

The tigers look disgusted at what they've detected, their noses crinkling.

What I smell crinkles my nose too: competing with Kelley's coconut-scented sunscreen is a mixture of compost bin and semen and manure—not the toxic kind like you can smell in Greeley feedlots, but an almost sweet, ripe, meaty manure. My dogs would go nuts, their nostrils dilating. Flocks of white seagulls dab at the waste piles.

We've arrived just at feeding time. Down below, at animal level, volunteers drive up in jeeps and toss what looks like roaster chickens over the fences into the tiger cages. Kelley and I watch the tigers lick chicken juice off the skin. They're dainty at first, and then they crunch the entire carcass on the side of their jaws. Then we realize that the chicken is just the distraction—the appetizer—to the big hunks of meat coming in. I'm a fairly small woman, so these huge slabs of meat are almost as big as me. The tigers hold them in an embrace as they devour them with ease. I could be eaten just as casually.

According to the tour guide, these tigers, all captive-born and -raised, come from abusive conditions. Ricky and Savannah, for example, lived in a horse trailer in Kansas for five years. Meeka and her mother Tajah were kept chained by the neck in a backyard in Minnesota. Many of the Bengal and Siberian tigers were purchased as cute, tiny cubs, but then surrendered when their owners found they could no longer feed and shelter their 500- to 850-pound beasts. Most had been kept in small concrete-and-steel cages, causing joint troubles, and were malnourished if not starving. When illegally owned exotics got injured or sick, the owners often failed to get veterinary help for fear of losing their animals. Some of the tigers were not surrendered but confiscated. Owners who clearly could not handle their animal burden nevertheless moved from state to state to dodge laws put up to block them. These owners couldn't bear to live without the animals they so loved and abused. Many of these owners, it seems, thought *they* were running sanctuaries, and would do nearly anything to "save" their animals from confiscation. I'm beginning to suspect that the impulse to hoard and the impulse to rescue may not be as distinct as depicted in the TWAS literature.

The stereotype of the exotic animal owner today is the sadistic drug lord with the chained tiger or the greedy circus owner who abuses his animals purely for money and then abandons them when they're no longer profitable. These cases certainly exist, but they're not, research suggests, the most common. At least as numerous are the hoarders.

Now increasingly understood as a mental illness, exotic animal hoarding has been linked with other forms of hoarding. Hoarding Disorder (HD) is now an official diagnosis in the DSM-5. Although animal hoarding is not listed as a subtype, many mental health researchers find most cases of animal hoarding to fit well within this diagnostic classification, which also links it with Obsessive-Compulsive Disorder (OCD). It's not the number of animals kept that defines animal hoarding, but their condition. Multiple animal ownership becomes hoarding when a person can no longer provide proper nutrition or sanitation. Usually, the hoarder fails to see the abuse caused by such conditions, even when animals are starving and disease-ridden, or even living among dead animals whose carcasses have not been removed.

Statistically, hoarders of exotic animals are more likely to be male. They're closely related, though, to the statistically female hoarders of domestic animals, most commonly dogs and cats. I get that chill of strange familiarity, similar to the one over the Zanesville incident, when I hear of the old widow found with dozens of malnourished cats in her house, the sting of ammonia in the air so pungent that Animal Control rescuers require gas masks. Or the woman whose private rescue shelter got out of hand after she could no longer keep up with the care and feeding of her fifteen dogs, but couldn't bear to give any up, had to be restrained while the animals were forcibly taken. Such hoarders love their animals beyond measure, beyond reason. Wrong as they are, they truly believe they are rescuers.

I get hints of how they feel when, from time to time, I scan the websites of animal shelters to see what new dogs are up for adoption. Just to look. There are always more dogs than "forever homes," and I understand the urge, deeper than hunger, to save them all.

Farther along the TWAS bridge, I hear another father say to his son, "Look, that wolf looks like he's waking up." When the son asks his dad why, the dad replies, "Because he wants to eat you."

The wolves begin to rouse and move. They look arthritic as they walk with a deliberate placing of legs—until they run, and then they're all grace. I feel like I do when I visit the dog pound; I'm falling in love with all of them, so huge and dignified, even in their agitated scratching of fur shedding in clumps. These Arctic wolves, timberwolves, and wolf hybrids move like my husky mix and stare like my border collie, but more grandly and with more maturity. My own dogs now seem so juvenile and disappointing. At the same time I feel a twinge of guilt for keeping my dogs confined in my house and yard. Why is keeping dogs as pets okay when keeping wolf hybrids as pets is abuse? Am I already an animal abuser, enslaving my dogs, who, incidentally, are spending the day in doggie day camp so that I can prowl TWAS?

I overhear a little girl say, "Mommy, I want a pet wolf."

The mother replies, "Wolves aren't meant to be pets."

Her older brother adds, "You can get a dog that looks just life a wolf, it's called an Alaskan Malamute. Or also Husky."

"No," the girl insists. "I want a wolf."

I understand. I, too, want.

By the time of my Terry Thompson obsession I was down to three dogs, one dying of congestive heart failure, but at my most expansive I had four dogs and two cats. If I hadn't poured a good chunk of my income into their upkeep and veterinary care, I'd already have been in hoarding territory. As a middle-aged widow living alone, I fit the typical profile of domestic animal hoarder too perfectly. My life partner died a decade earlier, leaving me—as my friends with children would call my state—"childless." My obsessive-compulsive tendencies (self-diagnosed) then fixed on dogs. I'd already had three spaniel mixes. Each new dog I rescued was a little more of a challenge, a little closer to feral. Rescuing now became my calling.

I'd adopted Olive, dog number four, after a trip to the Humane Society to donate the toys my three geriatric canines no longer chased. I briefly considered adopting the dingo who was literally climbing the walls, but when a border collie hexed me with her stare, I took her home. She'd come from a hoarder with eight dogs, who was forced to surrender four of them. I would now have four dogs myself (not to mention the cats).

Olive's history of being tied to a tree all day long soon manifested itself in extreme territorialism and "resource protectiveness," requiring hundreds of dollars in training to counteract. That's when I learned I had to understand the dog's point of view, her sense of space, of boundaries, of scent, of movement, of threatening and submissive behaviors, which opened up whole new realms of perception to me. As I entered this mysterious world of signs and territories, though, Olive even more quickly learned to function in the human-headed society of my household. Though she never lost her resource protectiveness around strange dogs—that sudden lunge, that eye—the worst of her anxieties were tamed.

After two of my geriatric dogs died, I began scanning dog rescue websites again ("just to look"). On bad days I scanned animal shelter websites like an addict, looking for new, more desperate rescues. That's when I found a wolfy-looking beast named Tiger, an unsocialized stray found roaming a six-lane highway in Texas. He turned out to be wild in a different way from Olive. The first three times I took him to the dog park he jumped the fence and ran into the woods. When he did stay inside the fence, he grabbed the scruffs of other dogs' necks and pulled, swinging his powerful neck to and fro, a move wolves use to break the spines of prey. He jumped up on dining tables and countertops, knowing no bounds. He especially liked to gnaw on human arms like a puppy does, but with two-year-old teeth. I slathered Neosporin over my arms and began clicker training. Within a few months, Tiger settled into a "good dog," obeying all my commands and walking solicitously at my side, with only an occasional lunge at an unneutered male or an extended howl at the living room window. By then I missed his wildness. Jack London's Buck notwithstanding, though, there's no going back.

But dogs, domesticated animals, only hint at wildness. I wondered what it would be like to keep a truly wild and untamable animal. For a time, I was tempted to try a wolf hybrid, even though the ones I've seen in the dog park have been so reserved, so distant. They don't want to be touched, and disappear from under you when you go to pet them. They have no dog body language whatsoever—no relaxed-jaw dog-smile, not even a play bow past early puppyhood—and don't heed invitations of the frolicking dogs around them. These are canines whose eyes can never be met. If you look directly at them, either they turn away, submissive, or they accept your challenge. I've only seen the latter happen once, and fortunately the owner grabbed the leash and pulled hard before his canine launched.

So, I knew animal longing: the golden eyes, the matted fur wild to be brushed, the unclipped nails clacking in their concrete cages as they paced. The fear growls. The raised ears slowly softening. The ecstasy of connecting with an animal who couldn't be reached.

Of course, hoarding dogs, or even dog-wolf hybrids, is not the same as hoarding lions and tigers. Dogs have at least ten thousand years of domestication taming their genes. Still, I was on the same spectrum as Terry Thompson. The spectrum of people with Animal Disorders.

In addition to our obsessive-compulsive tendencies and the sense of an absence in our lives needing to be filled, we share an abiding longing to connect across species. I don't believe we're simply substituting animals for the human relationships we're supposed to prefer. That's too simple. In my case, I started amassing animals when my husband was still alive, back when I was well-loved. No, we also crave the animality of animals, its twin familiarity and alienness, its uncanny portals into other worlds of knowing, other ways of experiencing the world. We find the otherness of animals infinitely fascinating, even sacred. We may be so overwhelmed with our love for our animals, and our belief that only we can care for them properly, that we can't see how we're harming them.

We are the people who find the death of a tiger at least as tragic as that of a human. Maybe more. Valuing other species over our own, we may be evolutionary errata, if not outright pathological. Stronger than our longing for survival and self-preservation is our longing to love something wild, to connect with a consciousness unfathomable to us.

I can't begin to imagine how Terry Thompson managed fifty-plus exotics for as long as he did. At the time of the Zanesville catastrophe, my six pets were all domesticated animals under thirty-five pounds. Even so, tending to all their needs—feeding them, walking them, giving them physical and mental stimulation, keeping their shots up to date, cutting their nails while they screamed bloody murder and made me expect Animal Control at my door—drained me physically, emotionally, and financially. Much as I loved my animal family, there were days when it felt like they were eating me alive. And my dogs and cats weren't even wild.

Down to two dogs now, I've had to ban myself from prowling the dog rescue websites. Because how do you know when you've crossed the line and become captive to your desire? How do you stop before your transspecies desire consumes you?

Now, after more spectators have arrived at TWAS, I can feel the bridge shaking under me. It could break, and I could fall into the animal dens. If it happens, I'm thinking, it's probably best to get attacked by a tiger. That would be quick. I've seen videos of lions where they start eating a cow while it's still alive and lowing. On the other hand, the tigers were freshly fed, so they might toy with me cat-and-mouse style.

Kelley and I return to the tigers. It's the tigers who most awe me with their total otherness, their monstrosity. And yet, there's something familiar about them too, something that grabs hold of you. I begin to feel something like sympathy, even kinship. I watch one tigress, like a house-cat, lick her paws with eyes closed, then rub them over ears. For a few seconds the ear folds dog-ear-style before flapping back into its upright position. I imagine Terry Thompson felt closest to his tigers, with their expressionless faces and hieroglyphic bodies.

According to the TWAS literature, some of these tigers came from Terry Thompson's zoo in Zanesville, though I'd read elsewhere that all eighteen of his tigers were shot, along with all seventeen of his lions. Thompson must have known his animals would be killed if he set them free. So why did he do it? Some people have said he wanted revenge on the community hounding him to curtail his menagerie. Others have said the government was closing in on him for his illegal gun collection. Some labeled him simply insane (as if insanity were ever simple). Others called him evil. Many believed he hated his animals, and his releasing them to their certain deaths was the ultimate act of hatred.

But I never accepted these charges. Obviously, I've been projecting onto the other Thompson, but seeing these tigers now makes me even more convinced. I believe he loved them in the most tragically, pathologically dysfunctional of ways, with the ultimate impossible love, unrequited and unrequitable. When I imagine him on his last day, he's filled with longing and sorrow for his creatures. He may have hated humans at that point, but not his beloved animals. Maybe, feeling caged himself, he over-identified with them, and wanted to give them the taste of wild freedom, at least for one brief moment, that he could never have. Because nothing will cage you more absolutely than keeping exotic animals. When Thompson's body was discovered, one of his tigers was ravaging his remains. The possessive desire for wildness can eat you alive.

In Werner Herzog's documentary *Grizzly Man*—perhaps the most famous documentary of an Animal Disorder—Timothy Treadwell, who spent over a decade of summers living among Alaskan bears, says several times into the camera, "I will die for these animals." He explains that if they attack, "I will be one of them." In manic ecstasy he touches a bear's fresh excrement and exclaims, as if identifying with the feces, "I was inside her!" (Holy shit, indeed.) At points he even wants to become more bear than human: "I have to mutually mutate into a wild animal."

To experience, as a human, what it's like to be nonhuman: that may be the ultimate metaphysical paradox. I wonder if that's why so many religions solve this paradox through mythological creatures, impossibly part-human and part-animal: sphinxes, fauns, satyrs, centaurs, mermaids, elephant gods, and fallen angels incarnated as serpents. Or sometimes as creatures who metamorphose from human to animal. In Ovid's *Metamorphoses*, Actaeon, hunter of deer, himself turns into an ungulate, horns sprouting from his head as he hears his baying dogs approach. It's what many hunters say hunting gives them: the necessity to think like both predator and prey. They experience the wildness and animal exigencies of these nonhuman species.

Contemporary American pop culture offers its own pantheon of human-animal hybrids: Spiderman, Batman, Catwoman, and an infestation of werewolves and blood-sucking vampires. These freakish monsters demonstrate, at least to me, something of the desire for "becoming-animal" (to borrow French philosopher Gilles Deleuze's term). The word "demonstrate" derives from the same root as "monster," and monsters can show us our subterranean selves. But they also show us something not-self. These monsters may demonstrate our impossible desire to know the world as only a non-human animal can know it.

In real life, such hybridity is impossible; the human dies in its transformation to animal. Actaeon, turning into a stag, is in the same instant attacked by his own hunting dogs and mauled out of existence. Timothy Treadwell only became bear in death; at the end of his thirteenth summer of peaceful coexistence with bears, one of them attacked Treadwell and his girlfriend, Amie Huguenard. Their remains were later found in the digestive tract of the suspected grizzly, killed as part of the investigation. Treadwell's fantasy of being inside a bear, or of metamorphosing into one, was eerily realized. However, his love of bears killed not only two human beings but at least one ursine being as well. That's what happens when a person tries to "become animal."

Ultimately, animal wildness is always beyond reach. The desire to connect with something wild is a doomed and dooming desire; the very act of connection contaminates the otherness and the wildness, and often the animal itself. It's an unstable, untenable contradiction, this tragic, dysfunctional love, unrequited and unrequitable. I imagine these deeply paradoxical urges consuming Terry Thompson.

So this is how I understand Terry Thompson: driven not (or not *only*) by a will to power but (also) by fascination, by a perverted reverence—a longing to cross species and become part of a non-human family, to be raised by other animals, to submit to their animality, in all its alienness as well as its startling familiarity. More mind-altering than hallucinogens, this animality opens onto other worlds of knowing, other ways of sensing and experiencing. What does it mean to think through smell, as my dogs do, or to hear ultrasonic stirrings, or to sense the earth's magnetic pull? People driven by this curiosity, this hunger, find the otherness of animals not just fascinating but *sacred*. What, after all, is a religious experience, if not a radical humbling before a force much greater than ourselves, a force that is ultimately unknowable?

In the end Thompson, like Treadwell, was perversely metamorphosed into his animals at death, becoming one with them. Apparently he spread the remains of a dead chicken on himself to attract his animals to his body, which may be why police discovered Thompson's corpse as it was being devoured by a tiger. Maybe this is what he wanted, this literal incorporation. It may be the only way a person can truly become animal.

Still, that photo from October 2011 continues to haunt me. It's the image I've been seeking to displace, but even now it overpowers the sight of these healthy tigers before me. That famous photograph that slipped from Zanesville to the world, in which rows of massive tiger and lion carcasses cover the killing fields. It's still as hard for me to look at as the piles of human corpses in a concentration camp photo. So while I'd like to believe that some of these animals are Zanesville survivors, giving me that sliver of a positive ending to the Thompson story, I know there can be no genuinely happy ending to keeping exotics captive.

But still. These tigers can hold a mysterious spell over a person. They don't see or acknowledge the humans, don't care about us. It makes you want to woo them, to try to win them over, to put your hands on them and absorb some of their power. You want to know them and, in spite of everything, to love them.

Kelley and I stop again at the serval enclosure on the way out. Now that we've seen 350-pound lions and 800-pound tigers, these 35-pound servals look tiny, almost indistinguishable from housecats. A human could easily hold this feline in her arms and nuzzle its head under her chin.

The guides should give us an exit lecture even more stinging than the one we received upon on entry, a sharper excoriation of the evils of exotics ownership. It doesn't take long—no more than a two-hour walk over a bridge—to go from complete ignorance to a captivating desire.

"Look at them, so cute," Kelley squeals again, and then adds, more reverently, with the acquisitive longing he usually only reserves for Stickley furniture or van Briggle pottery, "I want one!"

I put my finger to my lips. I recognize the tone in his voice, and the need it attempts to restrain, but I know better than to express such desires. It must be what Terry Thompson felt, way back when he encountered his first big cat and dreamed of connection. Your longing grows fierce as hunger. The serval paces and paces. I could be the other Thompson. This is how it begins.

8/ Schrödinger's Dogs

In 1935, the physicist Erwin Schrödinger put a cat in a steel box with a vial of poisonous hydrocyanic acid and a radioactive source. The apparatus was rigged so that when the first atom decayed, it would trigger a hammer to break the vial and kill the cat. Since the time it took for the first atom to decay was a matter of random chance, and since opening the box to find out if the cat were still alive would automatically kill the cat (giving new meaning to the adage "curiosity killed the cat"), the observers outside the box could never know with certainty at any given moment whether the cat inside was alive or dead.

Schrödinger's experiment would be unlikely to pass an ethics review board today, at least not if the cat were real. At any rate, "Schrödinger's Cat" was only ever just a thought experiment, a kind of allegory demonstrating radical uncertainty in subatomic physics; no actual cats were harmed in its making.

I first encountered Schrödinger's cat, though, while researching nuclear radiation—real, actual radiation. Because my post-widowhood boyfriend is a radiation oncologist—he uses radiation to treat cancers that might have been caused by radiation in the first place—I've been trying to get a handle on how radiation works. I'm also a lover of cats and dogs and other mammals, so in a doggedly literal-minded mode, when I heard about Schrödinger's thought experiment, I kept thinking about the poor cat and not the inaccessible electron it represented.

In a way, though, isn't Schrödinger's cat an apt metaphor for all research animals, closed off in cages, their states of life or death uncertain, subordinated to the expansion of human knowledge?

I do a lot of my thinking in the dog park. My high-energy border collie and husky-terrier mutts both came with insatiable needs for exercise and mental stimulation, so we spend at least an hour every day in our dog park, one of the remaining bastions in my city where the residual beast in the dog can run unleashed. Walking inside its perimeter, I start my own thought experiment: if killing an actual cat—or a dog—were necessary to advance our understanding of nuclear physics, would it be worth it? Would I be able to "sacrifice" on the altar of science even one of these Labradors or golden retrievers or—more likely—beagles scampering around me? And if not, what's the difference between these critters and their counterparts in laboratories, of the same species and equally capable of being someone's pet? (The ethics of pet-keeping itself—along with dog leashes, leash laws, spaying and neutering, and the daily doggie restrictions and humiliations that pets face—is another puzzle for another day.) What kinds of knowledge would, at least for me, be worth killing a non-human animal for, and how would I decide? What if the dog or cat had to suffer? How much suffering is worth how much knowledge?

I'm not alone in asking these questions, of course; animal researchers, veterinarians, philosophers, animal ethicists, and animal rights activists grapple with them daily, and their variant answers represent an aggregate uncertainty, even indeterminacy. We know, too, that the presence of the observer affects the observed, and that even thought experiments rarely occur in a vacuum. What if Schrödinger had posed his theoretical question before an observing cat, or if animal researchers posed theirs in a dog park?

Just a few miles northwest of my dog park, on Colorado State University's Foothills Campus in Fort Collins, a collection of research beagles was kept from the 1960s to the 1980s. I recently learned about this "beagle colony" while reading about the history of radiation, and for some reason it's been dogging me ever since. For me, the ghosts of the research beagles now hover over the dog park.

The Collaborative Radiological Health Animal Research Laboratory (CRHARL), nicknamed "Charlie lab," tested the long-term effects of radiation on mammals. They chose beagles as the test animal because of the breed's "pleasant disposition and convenient size." Some two thousand beagles were irradiated and observed for several decades along with their offspring, many irradiated in utero. These observations produced important data not only on the late effects to be expected in human victims exposed to radiation (such as in the Hiroshima and Nagasaki bombings), but also on the use of radiation therapy to treat cancerous tumors. Drs. William Carlson, Robert Phemister, and Ed Gillette conducted research that helped lay the foundation for therapeutic uses of radiation today.

This beagle colony was once legendary in Fort Collins, in part because, as its former director Dr. C. W. Miller told me, "everybody knew when it was feeding time." The barking must have resounded along the foothills. The research complex included some thirteen hundred outdoor dog pens with culverts for cold weather. These roughly eight-by-eight-foot pens were made of special wire mesh screens whose sole purpose was to keep the set-up sterile. These dogs could see each other, and were sometimes paired in pens, so they weren't cut off from the world, as many laboratory dogs are. And, of course, they also had that twice-daily social interaction with handlers at feeding times. Indeed, I've been impressed by the pride the Charlie lab researchers still feel not only over the research produced but also over the care and treatment of the dogs.

Several people I talked to from the "Charlie lab" days laughed when they remembered how they had to shower down before entering the pens and to wash all the dog food in formalin, even though geese flew overhead, leaving their droppings behind and sometimes trying to steal the dog food. I imagine the dogs barking at the geese and the geese honking back. Maybe the goose visits even gave the beagles a hint of the hunt bred into their genes. Still, the dogs never got to feel the grass under their paws or to dig Colorado's thick, clay-like dirt. Dr. Bernie Rollin, a young CSU philosophy professor at the time and now a renowned animal ethicist, told me how people used to call him about the interminable beagle howling, whose accumulated boredom, anxiety, and need must have suggested animal torture.

In fact, Dr. Rollin told me, these beagles had it good relative to other lab experiments conducted on dogs at the time. The Charlie lab merely subjected the dogs to radiation and then monitored them into the next generation. Beagles used for other experiments were not so lucky, especially in the 1960s, before the Animal Welfare Act (AWA) of 1966 (Public Law 89-544). It was common in other research labs to perform surgery after surgery—even as many as nine surgeries—on a real beagle in the laboratory. Sometimes these surgeries were done without expense-adding anesthesia or painkillers. Dr. Rollin remembers "Frankendogs" with so many surgeries performed on them that their coats were more scar tissue than fur.

As FDA oversight tightened in the 1960s, requiring human-bound products to be proven safe, and the use of animals for scientific research and product testing expanded, questions about animal ethics bred like rabbits. At one extreme of the animal rights spectrum, so extreme that it's probably only theoretical, is the belief that all animals have rights and every animal matters as much as every other. PETA resides somewhere toward the end of this end of the long tail. At the other extreme, any human interest outweighs any interest of animals. Most Americans fall somewhere in between; we might grant that some animals should have some rights, and some (such as family dogs, as well as the primates most resembling our own species) may approach or even attain the level of "personhood," but we might still privilege human needs and desires over those of other animals.

The AWA was introduced in the 1960s, an era when dogs moved indoors, snuck onto the living room sofa, and nosed their way into the American family. No longer merely the hunters, workers, and guards they were bred to be, they became pets and companions and even family members. The primary impetus for the AWA was less the reduction of suffering of research animals and more the protection of people's family dogs against being stolen and sold to laboratories. This happened most famously to a Dalmatian named Pepper, who, according to the 1965 account of this dognapping in *Sports Illustrated*, ended up dying in the laboratory before his devastated human family could recover him. The Act even opens by acknowledging this motivation:

> *Be it enacted by the Senate and House of Representatives of the United States of America in Congress assembled.* That, in order to protect the owners of dogs and cats from theft of such pets, to prevent the sale or use of dogs and cats which have been stolen...

In 1966, on the heels of *Sports Illustrated*'s Pepper story, *Life Magazine* ran an article titled "Concentration Camp for Dogs," which revealed gruesome laboratory conditions. The Act took on this wrongdoing, too, continuing:

> ...and to insure that certain animals intended for use in research facilities are provided humane care and treatment, it is essential to regulate the transportation, purchase, sale, housing, care, handling, and treatment of such animals by persons or organizations engaged in using them for research or experimental purposes or in transporting, buying, or selling them for such use. (https://www.nal.usda.gov/awic/animal-welfare-act-public-law-89-544-act-august-24-1966)

Our new "humane care and treatment" of laboratory dogs (among other *certain* animals," but excluding agricultural animals, mice, and rats) depended on their becoming honorary humans. We couldn't allow our beloved dogs to be nabbed; they were family, so we were pained by their pain. To the extent that they were humanized, dogs' lives mattered.

After the AWA conditions improved, at least on paper, for research dogs and some other laboratory species. Further improvements came with subsequent amendments (see *United States Code,* Title 7, Sections 2131-2156). With the 1985 addition, referred to as the "Improved Standards for Laboratory Animals Act," conditions of "sanitation, housing, and ventilation" now had to meet specific standards of "humane care." The amended AWA also required "exercise for dogs and an adequate physical environment to promote the psychological well-being of non-human primates"—a requirement my own dogs have imposed on me. The amended AWA further ruled "that pain and distress must be minimized in experimental procedures and that alternatives to such procedures be considered by the principle investigator," and restricted research to "one major operative experiment with recovery" per animal (with exceptions). Operating on animals repetitively or without adequate anesthesia became banned. Further, the use of research animals had to be justified by the experiment's potential benefits. That's what the law says, anyway, though some of my friends in the field say otherwise.

Currently, scientific experiments on dogs at U.S. research institutions get screened by an oversight committee, the IACUC (Institutional Animal Care and Use Committee), consisting of a veterinarian, a scientist, a nonscientist unaffiliated with the institution, and a chairman. Any project receiving NIH (National Institutes of Health) or other government funding (which covers nearly all university studies) must follow *The Guide for the Care and Use of Laboratory Animals,* or "The Guide." According to The Guide, researchers should find alternatives to "whole-animal testing" whenever possible. When whole-animal testing is required, NIH and FDA guidelines advocate maximizing the yield of useful data with the minimum number of animals and that they employ the most "humane" methods possible.

"In theory," my veterinary friends tell me. Practice doesn't always match theory.

If I'm being honest, I would have to place myself among the majority of Americans in the middle of the ethical spectrum. I'm uncomfortable with needless animal cruelty in laboratory settings, but I also recognize the need for some degree of animal testing, and acknowledge that I have benefitted greatly from animal testing that would make me uncomfortable (as pretty much all of us do every time we take a pill or apply a lotion). I probably would have cringed at seeing those thousands of beagles penned up for a lifetime beside foothills they could never roam. Still, I decide in the dog park, from everything I've learned, the Charlie lab work seems to me justified and, well, "humane" (a term whose anthropocentric bias is itself telling). Since loved ones of mine have benefited from oncological radiation treatments, which were enabled in part by Charlie lab and related research, I can only be thankful to those two thousand beagles.

At the same time, though, I would never subject my own dogs to needless surgery or irradiation, no matter what knowledge was to be gained. In our dog park, a short run from the historical Charlie lab, I meet many beagles, some of whom have come through a major rescue shelter for laboratory beagles located just north of us in Wyoming. When I bend to pet these beagles, their caramel eyes meet mine and recognize me as a distinct living being. I have a hard time sentencing them to suffering on my species' behalf.

A former CSU police officer from the Charlie lab days told me that once, when she was doing a routine drive through the facility, her headlights caught a beagle puppy wiggling his way out of the enclosure. "I thought a lot of things in the moment, like if I leave him out here, he'll have no food or water and a coyote is probably going to get him. And I can't take him home because I'd probably lose my job over it. And if I push his little body back through the hole in the fence, they'll continue to do who-knows-what to him." It was a painful moment for this police officer as she lifted the little puppy, "all soft and silky," and stuffed him headfirst back into the pen. "His tail was wagging the whole time."

Leaving the dog park, I see the "big A" painted by university alums and boosters on the first mountain of the foothills, just beyond the fields where the Charlie lab once lay. Colorado State University, once Colorado A&M, originated as an agricultural college, with a still-enduring tradition of painting a giant white A on the mountainside every fall. A former worker at the Charlie lab told me that of all the two thousand dogs, only one ever tried to bite. When this dog bit the man's arm as the man entered the kennel, the gate door still open, the man realized he could only save either his arm or the dog, but not both. He chose his arm. "The last I saw of that dog," the man told me, "he was running up toward the big A."

This tame and docile beagle, lacking basic survival skills, was most likely running to his death. Those hills crawled with coyotes and poisonous snakes and all sorts of parasites. Nature is far crueler than laboratory conditions, defenders of research on colony-bred animals sometimes say. We'll never know when the beagle died or how long he survived. But I prefer to imagine that for one brief period, he was running free, kicking up grass with paws that felt its cushioning leaves for the first time, smelling the wild terrestrial possibilities rising up beneath those ground-stirring ears, and getting at least a taste of freedom. The other irradiated dogs may be suspended between life and death, but for this brief moment, the escaped dog was entirely, determinedly alive. I imagine him running still, away from the institution of knowledge and into the unknown.

I prefer this scenario to the one I know to be true: "justified" experiments and tests on dogs continue. Even today, between 60,000 and 75,000 dogs, primarily beagles, are used each year for testing. That could make for a lot of unheard howling. (The exact figure has become even harder to come by since 2017, when, under the head of Donald Trump's appointee Sonny Perdue, the USDA scrubbed these kinds of reports from its website, creating a whole new kind of uncertainty.)

Schrödinger tried, with his imaginary cat, to show the discrepancy between quantum physics, in which a subatomic particle can seemingly be in multiple locations at the same time, and conventional physics, in which something can only be in one place at one time, and in one state at one time—that is, in which a cat can be either alive or dead, but not both. Schrödinger wanted his allegory to illustrate the triumph of common sense over the non-Newtonian superposition theory, but other thinkers have celebrated the thought experiment's illustration of radical uncertainty.

Many people resort to "common sense" when it comes to animal ethics, and their common sense tells them that human lives matter more than dogs'. But my personal animal ethics also recognize the less common logic of quantum physics. Radical uncertainty is where I'm left in my own thought experiment. Or maybe, in my case, "radical uncertainty" is just a euphemism for hypocrisy. I do want my drugs tested on mice at least, and possibly on dogs, since the latter are much better models of human physiology. But not on my own dogs. And I want that suffering sealed off in a black box, as invisible to me as an orbiting electron is to nuclear physicists, or as Schrödinger's cat is to its human observers.

9/ Pack Theory

"No!" I growled at Tiger, who was humping his big sister, Olive, in the back seat of my car. These two dogs and I had existed peaceably together for years. Then, a couple weeks ago, I took in Buster, a three-year-old Aussie-terrier mix, from a colleague who couldn't keep up with his insistent needs. I thought I could foster him for a while. That's when Tiger's humping began. If you bring a new dog into a pack, the whole intricate flowchart of power relations has to be redrawn.

This new humping-for-hierarchy started on the December morning of the first of three days of interviews my English department colleagues and I were conducting by Skype. We were hiring a new assistant professor in creative nonfiction, with me as the chair of the search committee. I'd woken up early to give the dogs an hour in the dog park before my long day of back-to-back interviews. These morning canine sessions in the dog park usually helped me fill my emotional reservoir for the day ahead, but that Tuesday morning, Olive's behavior was disheartening. She had always been my belligerent bitch, a reactive-aggressive border collie who first snarled and then lunged at any dog venturing anywhere near her butt. Today, though, when Tiger, with all his husky-terrier alacrity, executed his symbolic exertions, she just stood there and took it.

My search committee was a dream team of particularly collegial colleagues in an uncharacteristically collegial English department. Even so, a team is always, elementally, a pack. It's a weird thing, chairing a committee whose task is to hire a younger, better version of yourself. In this case my department was looking for someone who could lead the program I'd helped develop but had been unable to raise into the kind of national prominence that a bolder, more energetic and visionary new colleague might achieve.

Some of my search committee members already had that kind of visionary energy and assertive authority that I could never claim. They were the real deal. Of course, they didn't have to *say* they were the real deal; they just assumed that "calm assertiveness" that Cesar Millan, the "Dog Whisperer," extols: that attitude of alpha dogs that renders the others submissive without needing any overt violence. For dogs, Cesar says, it's all about pack ranking; the human needs to "be the pack leader." Millan's theory of dog training is controversial; animal behaviorists and ethologists (who study how animals interact in their natural environments rather than under artificial conditions) almost uniformly dismiss his theory of pack behavior as naïve and outdated. I haven't studied canine ethology much beyond observations of my own pack, but in my experience Millan's model applies best to humans. This December day found me submissive around my clearly superior colleagues, tucking tail and averting my gaze when they praised the candidates whose work I found too preciously clever and dismissed my favorite candidate as insufficiently charismatic to compete with students' hand-held electronics. Their assertions of surety confirmed to me once again that they were the real writer-scholars, the pros, and I was the amateur, the con.

For all eight hours on Day One the five of us search committee members huddled in a glass-walled room in the university library, exposed like puppies in a pet store window. While we Skype-interviewed, a blizzard rolled in. Outside, the trees' networks of branches turned to white lace before moaning under the snow's weight. By the time I left the library the snow reached my knees, overtopping my boots. The ever-diligent Facilities staff had plowed the parking lot but not the snowdrifts forming flying buttresses around our cars. I shuffled to mine, feeling the snow's resistance in my right hip joint, the one with the cartilage ground away so that the ball scraped against its socket. I knew what this stiff walk looked like; Olive, my aging black border collie, had started showing signs of this same malady in the dog park. She tried to fake it when someone was watching, but limped outright when she believed herself unobserved. I now limped unobserved through the parking lot's whiteness, unable to lift my right leg over the drift thick as vanilla frosting at the car door. Olive would be swimming in the backyard snow by the time I got home, and then limping all evening, while Tiger and Buster were still sprightly enough to dolphin over the ocean of snow.

Retrieving the shovel from my trunk, I began burrowing my way out of my parking space. *Lift with your legs*, my back said in twinges. *Fuck that*, my knees rejoined. Snow had begun to drip down my calves and refreeze at my feet. I could feel my toes turning the blue-gray of the sky. It took me forty-five minutes to drive the ten-minute trip home. As I slid and skittered and prayed that my little Prius would clear the mounds of snow, I tried to calm myself by picturing the dogs waiting at the front window back home, their noses sliming the glass. Buster's red merle cuddliness, Tiger's bent head and manipulatively imploring eyes, Olive's bossy pack-keeping; they almost made me smile in spite of my bluing toes.

Instead, I got home to diarrhea all over the dining room floor, green and stinky and untreatable. My weary hipbones moaned as I scrubbed. Then I faced the raucous dog energy, and fighting when I went to feed them. Buster turned a blind eye, while Olive and Tiger tore into each other and I pulled them apart. Tiger had never even snarled before (unless I tried to brush his tail). I didn't get it. Then I figured out what was going on: they were re-negotiating power and status. At nearly nine years old (roughly the dog equivalent of my fifty-two human years, euphemized as "middle age"), Olive was being replaced by the five-year-old (or thirty-something) Tiger. The disruption of a new dog in the pack instigated this re-evaluation, confirming that even the toughest of us, when we reach middle age, are no longer alpha material. And I, unlike Olive, have never been the toughest of us.

The snow bloviated all night long, so before making my way to campus for Day Two of Skype interviews, I had to shovel a foot of snow from my sidewalk and driveway. It took two hours. I got more and more annoyed with Rajiv as my back torqued and my quads burned. On his urging, we'd bought the house together after he promised to always mow the lawn, rake all the leaves, and shovel all the snow. Then, barely a year after we bought the house, he was diagnosed, at age thirty-seven, with terminal cancer, and a year later he was dead. Every time I shoveled, especially now that I'd gone arthritic, I cursed him for betraying me, even as my burning muscles and throbbing joints made me miss him all the more, miss him, even after thirteen years, with the intensity of fresh loss.

The dogs watched me from the window, warm and dry. When I came in, they were full of energy and play, but there was no time to go to the dog park; I'd used that time doing Rajiv's shoveling.

I tried to be assertive as leader of the search committee, but my colleagues just talked louder, blustering over me, and by the end of the day I found myself deferring to their greater authority. At the very end of an afternoon Skype interview, we heard a bark. "I'm sorry about my dog," the candidate said. I broke into a smile and started to speak, but before I could, three other voices piled on top of mine. That had been going on all day, but this was my territory.

"This city is a great place for dogs," one committee member—who had no interest whatsoever in dogs—jumped in.

"Very dog-friendly here," another dogless member added.

"I have a dog," a third out-shouted, "and I can attest to what a good place this is for dog lovers."

"I have three dogs," I finally inserted, slower than the others, but staking my claim nonetheless, "and I—"

"Alright now," the department chair said before we lost all professional credibility. "Enough of that now."

Later, I left the room feeling huffy. The others could interrupt me on anything else, but dogs were mine. My colleagues didn't wake up at 5:00 A.M. to spend an hour slugging through dog park snowdrifts at fifteen degrees. They didn't organize their lives around the size of a dog's bladder, or sacrifice travel, or live as the minority species in a pack, or face a daily onslaught of collective collie-husky-terrier-Aussie energies. They're not the crazy lady of the dog park. That's my job.

As I drove home, though, embarrassment set in over my petty need to one-up my colleagues and claim dogs as my territory. A "calm assertive" leader wouldn't need to do that. Besides, it was actually less than half an hour I'd spent the previous morning amid the paw-printed snowdrifts, and I'd missed that second morning entirely.

On Day Three the blizzard left, deepening the cold. Snow solidified to ice on the roads. In the dog park, the dogs slid around on the rocks, unable to get a foothold. Later, in the library, we humans conducted the last four interviews, now so sick of our own enthusiasm that what had felt authentic at the start now degenerated into self-quotation; we merely recited the words of the people we used to be two days earlier. We were tired, and with all fourteen candidates strong, we knew we still had a struggle ahead of us.

That night after slip-sliding home, I gathered together the rankings of all five committee members and made a chart on my computer. As I did, I pulled out my plastic baggie of leftover crumbs from the cookies a search member had shared, and munched at the keyboard, with Buster at my side and Tiger under the desk, each eyeing the other, both dogs salivating. When I dropped a crumb, they both dove in, and then viciously fought each other. Not play-fighting, but the snarling, blood-rushing, red-in-tooth-and-claw species of fighting. "No!" I shouted (not calm-assertive but anxious-angry), and pulled them apart, but not before they'd snarled against my leg and drawn blood. Mine. The veins around the contact point quickly swelled and bunched, as if some bizarre Amazonian insect had crawled under my skin. I tried to push the hematoma back down.

The next morning a three-inch circle of purple emblazoned my left thigh. Buster and Tiger refused to pass each other in the hallway. Each stood and stared the other down from his claimed territory. When it's just a low, underlying rumble, I can't always tell which dog is growling. The previous night I had thought Tiger, in his newfound alpha-dom, was the aggressor, but in the morning Buster was the one growling pre-emptively at Tiger, hackles raised, while Tiger put his ears back and looked away. But then Buster wouldn't go outside to pee while Tiger was out, and when I carried him outside he scrambled right back in. Maybe they, themselves, didn't know who was on top. It seemed they were still figuring their alphas and omegas.

Day Four's ranking session was tense. We each held fast to our favorite candidates and wouldn't give, instead squabbling over procedure. I tried to assert my method atop the grumbles. Slowly a ranked list emerged. We tinkered. We tinkered a little more. Finally we agreed we could all live with it. We presented the list to the Executive Committee and the Office of Equal Opportunity representative, who quickly approved it. When the department chair publically thanked me for my fair and democratic leadership, and everyone clapped, some with tight necks and twitching lips, all I could hear was the humming undertone of growls.

Back home at 2:00 p.m., after letting the dogs out, I got in my sleeping clothes—sweatshirt and cut-off sweatpants—and climbed into bed. It may have only been mid-afternoon, but I was done with the day. Propping the laptop against my thighs to check my email, I saw that the bruise, level with the screen, had bloomed into a giant purple pansy. Even though I'd gotten my top choice candidate, I'd left the meeting likewise bruised.

I also knew that any one of these candidates over whom we'd fought so hard would, upon arrival, dismiss me as a has-been, privileged, middle-aged white woman. It was hard enough on the ego to listen to one after another of the bright rising stars for three days, their minds full of the new and cutting-edged, and uncluttered by the critical debates of decades past, into which I'd put years of study as a graduate student, and which were now quaint at best. Derrida was dead, and nobody cared about *différance* or *aporia*s or the absent presence anymore. Or that I had been a bright rising star once too. Now I could see this new batch of astral risers looking upon me the way I once looked upon my academic elders, as the ones in need of displacement. The real toppling was still to come.

After Rajiv died, my last round of dogs had reshuffled their hierarchy. When the funeral home workers wheeled Rajiv's body out our front door, Pretzel, who'd lived for Rajiv, crawled under the futon and refused to eat for days. A black cocker spaniel/border collie mix, Pretzel was then six years old, roughly the dog equivalent of my human thirty-nine. He'd always been dominant over his fellow spaniel mix, Chappy, then four. Almost overnight, it seemed—though my sense of time was askew with shock and grief—Pretzel's muzzle went white. When he'd crawled out from the futon, Chappy matter-of-factly mounted him. "No!" I'd growled as the humping commenced, but Chappy went at it with the stubbornness of instinct. When I pulled the opportunistic upstart off his elder, he re-mounted with more resolution, the whole force of nature behind him. I realized there was nothing I could do but let it happen. After Chappy's first few thrusts, Pretzel stopped fighting. Today even bossy Olive seems to know when to give up the fight.

Now, as I write this, the laptop propped against the purple blackwidow-sized bruise on my thigh, these second-round dogs have settled into bed with me, the aging Olive at my feet, Tiger and Buster on either side of my ribs, the way Chappy once did before he, too, grew old and got cancer. I can see new white hairs on Olive's once-black muzzle. "It's hard, isn't it, the life of an aging diva?" I say to her. She looks at me cautiously, distrustfully, even as I rub her exposed belly with a foot while the two boys burrow their heads into my armpits. All seems peaceable for the moment. I can't tell if these dogs are in a temporary cease-fire or if the power struggle has concluded. If the latter, I may never know who won.

A Bitchuary

Olive is dead.

But can such a dog die?

Her pink tongue, which was once blood red.

I arrived home to the stink of shit. She'd pooped on the dining room floor, and thrown up in the living room. There she lay, chin stretched out on the floor, not moving. Tiger kept scanning her body with probing sniffs, as if she smelled all wrong.

"Olive, up! Up, up, up!" I coaxed, but no.

I lifted her to her feet.

She slid back down. Licked her lips.

But the light was not yet out of her eyes.

She stared at me, her unblinking, uncompromising, unconditional Border collie stare.

I took her to urgent care.

The ultrasound showed her heart encased in fluid. A mass on her heart had burst. Hemangiosarcoma, almost surely. They could revive her, but she'd still have metastatic cancer.

So, no.

So, euthanasia.

They gave me the same "comfort room" that Pretzel, my first dog, had died in. As soon as I crossed the threshold I cried, even before they wheeled Olive in on a wagon.

They gave me some time alone with her.

Olive, do you know what's happening? Are you OK with it?

Pretzel had given me the OK. Chappy, too. Olive did not. The ferocity still burned in her black-brown eyes. The fight never left her lungs. She wasn't ready. She was dying, her tongue and gums going pale as her heart bled out, but still she wasn't ready.

When Rajiv was in liver failure, his brain stem already fogging, I'd asked him if he wanted to sign a "Do Not Resuscitate" form. "Can't you at least try?" he'd said.

Can't you at least try? Olive's eyes said.

I sobbed into her scruff.

Which she did not appreciate, not at all. She even stepped off the death wagon and tried to walk away from me. As if my crying were unseemly, or just plain annoying.

Olive stayed Olive to the end. Olive on her own terms.

When friends used to wonder what Olive was like as a puppy, I'd reply, "Olive was never a puppy." She arrived fully formed out of a bolt of lightning, a force of nature. Or she was Kali, the Hindu goddess, materialized as a fully-formed warrior out of the third-eye stare of Durga.

How can such a force die?

She who made puppies cry when they tried to lick her lips. She who never submitted. Who lived fully and furiously. More Fury than Muse. More live than love. More always than ever.

She who bossed and who bullied. Who berated and belabored, who moaned and bemoaned, who pulsed and compulsed. She who ate and who hated and who perseverated. Who charged, who thundered, who hungered. Who made her body an arrow. Who shot, who speared, who pierced, punctured, perforated, performed. Who evered. Who nevered. Who averred, asserted, endured.

She who verbed all adjectives, who left no nouns standing in her wake, who plowed through punctuation and snarled even at the final period.

She to whom the devil came in the form of a squirrel. She, the she-devil, whose shrieks punctured the devil's own eardrums. She who raided the devil's hoard of souls.

She who ever bore Kali's tongue, that red lolling tongue of the Hindu goddess bedecked with a necklace of skulls, that blood-dripping, ever-thirsty tongue.

"She might start to lick her lips when I inject the medicine," the emergency vet said. "Sometimes they do that."

Olive had always licked her lips when agitated.

"The medicine should relax her first, and then she'll just slip away."

But when the vet started injecting, Olive perked up, lifted her ears, tried to resist. And kept upright, and would not let go. Then finally her chin rested on the ground.

"Good girl," we all said at once, but she was already gone. I don't think she'd relaxed until after she was dead. Her away did not slip; it tore.

They let me stay with the body until I was "ready." I kept petting her. She didn't seem dead. She seemed poised to bolt. All the other dogs I'd euthanized, my three spaniel mixes, were definitely dead, their bodies relaxed into final rest. Olive's body seemed still tense and fighting even after death. Like she would lift her head any minute and glare at me.

In spite of all the despair, how I'd loved that bitch. Her intensity. Her fight. Her absolute, full-bodied, full-bloodied bitchiness.

She died with a slip of tongue sticking out, still licking her lips.

Acknowledgments

Many of the essays originally appeared in different forms in various venues:

"Consider the Hamster" appeared in part as "Consider the Hamster" in *Under the Sun*. http://www.uts2013.com/consider-the-hamster-2/ and in part as "Meta-Hamster." Under the Sun. (2016). http://Underthesunonline.com/wordpress/2016/meta-hamster/

"Big Cats" was originally published as "Risking Sentiment." *An Orange County Almanac: and other essays*. Ed. J. Zammit-Lucia. New York: Wolfoundation. 2013: 39-50.

"The Meaning of Meat" appeared in *The Briar Cliff Review*, Volume 24: 14-18, where it was the 2012 Nonfiction Contest winner.

"The Blue Heron Returns" is a combination of "Other Dead People," which appeared in *Alligator Juniper*, 2008: 61-4, and "Peripheral Visions," published in *Fourth Genre*, volume 12.1 (Spring 2010).

"See Monkey Dance, Make Good Photo" was published in *The Southeast Review*, 29.1: 172-180.

"For the Polar Bears" was first published as "Beefless" in *Creative Nonfiction*, Issue 41 (Spring 2011): 34-37.

"The Other Thompson" is a combination of an essay of that title, which appeared in *Barely South Review*, spring 2017 (http://Barelysouthreview. com/the-other-thompson/) and "Captivations," which appeared in *Better* #6 (http://bettermagazine.org/006/deborahthompson.html).

I owe a tremendous debt to the editors of these journals, as I do to the members of the Slow Sand Writers' Society, especially Jeana Burton, Jerry Eckert, Colleen Fulbright, Teresa Funke, Jean Hanson, Luana Heikes, Sara Hoffman, Paul Miller, Karla Oceanak, Leslie Patterson, Sue Ring deRosset, Kay Rios, Elisa Sherman, Greta Skau, and Melinda Swenson.

Thank you also to: the brilliant poet and teacher Veronica Patterson for sending me down this path; to Kelley Simpson, my emotional support human; to all my other emotional support animals (Kitty, Blinky, Lucky, Pretzel, Chaplin, Houdini, Olive, Tiger, and Penguin); to the Colorado State University Department of English, and especially my colleagues John Calderazzo, SueEllen Campbell, and Marnie Leonard, for supporting me in my creative nonfiction endeavors; and to Diane Goettel and Black Lawrence Press.

This book is dedicated to Ronald Thompson and Rajiv Bhadra.

Deborah Thompson is a Professor of English at Colorado
State University, where teaches literature and creative nonfiction. She has published numerous creative and critical
essays, and has won the *Missouri Review* and *Iowa Review*
awards in creative nonfiction, as well as a Pushcart prize.
She is the author of *Pretzel, Houdini, and Olive: Essays on
the Dogs of My Life*, published by Red Hen Press, and is
working on a nonfiction book on mythologies of dogs in
American culture.